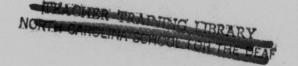

LISTEN TO
YOUR HEART

LISTEN TO YOUR HEART

A Message to Parents of Handicapped Children

Elise H. Wentworth

1974

HOUGHTON MIFFLIN COMPANY BOSTON

FIRST PRINTING   W

Library of Congress Cataloging in Publication Data

Wentworth, Elise H.
    Listen to your heart; a message to parents of handi-
capped children.

    Bibliography: p.
    1. Handicapped children. 2. Handicapped children—
Family relationships. I. Title.
HV888.W46   362.7′8′4   74–1341
ISBN 0–395–18494–0

For Kathy,
who taught me to listen to my heart,

Wayne,
who gave me the courage to listen to my heart,

Randall, Gregg, and Rick,
who teach my heart what to say.

There are many people whose help I gratefully acknowledge and two who were particularly helpful. The Reverend Mr. Charles F. Hood, rector of my parish, who helped me through many rough spots as I struggled to learn to accept my daughter as she is, who urged me to begin this book, then prodded and encouraged me to finish it, and served as consultant for the chapter concerning religion. Dr. Louis Fabre, Jr., whose work with the Texas Research Institute of Mental Sciences included parent counseling, willingly offered me his advice about the reactions parents of handicapped children experience.

Most of all, I would like to acknowledge the inestimable help given me by the most important consultants — the mothers and fathers of handicapped children who read the manuscript in various stages of development and offered their comments and suggestions.

Preface

A WEALTH OF help is available to parents who have handicapped children, but regardless of the counsel they may receive, it is the parents themselves who must ultimately make the decisions concerning their children's welfare. Parents have a built-in ability to be good mothers and fathers for their handicapped children, but all too often their capability becomes buried beneath the confusion built up by their fears and doubts.

Much has been written and many studies have been conducted about the parent–handicapped child relationship; thousands of teachers and counselors have been well trained in how to work with families of handicapped children, but the emphasis is usually placed upon helping the parents so that the child will be helped. That must be done, but what about the parents themselves? Where can a parent find the counsel he needs to help himself sort out the emotional reactions that this catastrophe arouses?

The purpose of this book is to help parents find courage, and the ways to break through that veneer of self-doubt, so they can find faith in their own capability.

You will listen to other people advise you about your problems, and often their advice will be very good, but the doubt will sneak into your thoughts, "How do *you* know how I feel? All you say and know is from what others have said." I know because I have asked the same question. Although I was trained in child psychology and education of exceptional children and have counseled parents of handicapped children throughout the years, I speak with the knowledge I have gained by being the mother of a mentally retarded and physically handicapped daughter. (And also as the mother of three *very* normal sons.) I, too, have felt the negative emotional reactions parents of handicapped children experience, and have sought help for myself, but found none available. Yet, I know that given a little help and a lot of encouragement, one can pull oneself out of the valley of depression, for I have seen many other parents do just that.

I know, too, the terrible strain that is put on a marriage when a child is handicapped. And, I also know how strong a marriage can become in love and respect when husband and wife earnestly try to understand and help each other.

This is a general, overall look at the problems most parents must solve when they have a child who is handicapped. The information offered is not comprehensive, because it is not directed to parents whose children are handicapped by a particular type of deficiency. The emotional reactions discussed are those that parents of any handicapped child must learn to overcome. Primarily, it is directed to parents who must learn to live with their handicapped children, at least during the childhood years.

I hope you will find the help here that you need for strengthening your courage and your faith in your own ability to be a good parent. Listen to your heart, for it is your inner voice of wisdom speaking.

Contents

PART II
ADJUSTMENT

THE ROAD
TO ACCEPTANCE

OF ALL THE BURDENS parents carry, the heaviest is that of having a child who is handicapped. The very fact that a child is deficient in the level of mental or physical ability which is considered to be normal, means that his parents are faced with unique problems — problems which at times can be overwhelming. Those of us who are parents of handicapped children know that one does survive the catastrophe, that the burdens can be lightened and the problems can be overcome.

We know, too, that the day you learned that your child is handicapped stands out as the darkest day in your life as a parent. It makes little difference whether this news came as a surprise or as a confirmation of your suspicions and fears built up over several years; whether the deficiency is of a smaller or a greater extent; whether this condition is a result of a birth injury, or an illness, or accident — you feel as if your world has ended.

In many ways your world did end, for when a child is handicapped the entire life pattern of the parents is changed. Whether the deficiency is mental or physical or a combination, you no longer can expect to know the fulfillment of your hopes and dreams for your child. That sunshine-filled life you had envisioned has disappeared, and now you feel that you can see only a dark wilderness ahead; you are afraid because of the strangeness. You do not want to believe it is true, and yet you must. Your happiness and your child's happiness depend upon how well you accept him as he is.

Basically, your job as a parent will be little different from that of parents of nonhandicapped children, since the basic aim of good parenthood still will apply — to provide a loving, happy home in which your child will gain a foundation of security that will insure his future happiness.

Now, at this beginning, you stand at one of the major crossroads in your life. Which of the two diverging paths you decide to follow is your choice, for although others may advise you, the decision is yours alone to make. Neither path is smooth, yet the one that is marked Rejection leads to the dark gloom of despair, while the other path leading to Acceptance will carry you to that destination which is the ultimate goal — good adjustment.

Just what does acceptance mean, and what is it all about? Dictionaries define the word as: "to admit, to take as true, to take with good grace; to bear up under in a resigned or patient manner; to acknowledge or admit as having existence." Acceptance, then, is admitting that your child is handicapped because of his lack of ability and realizing the true limits of his capability. Acceptance is also acknowledging the fact that your life will be different from that which you had expected and anticipated as being a parent.

The development of acceptance is a long-time and often a difficult process, since it involves every facet of the personality. Much will be determined by the attitudes and feelings that you developed over the years and carried with you from childhood into adulthood. You will learn much about yourself, and you will learn to be honest with what is revealed. You will discover the good that is within you and how to expand that good, and you will discover that you must discard what is bad. You will have to decide for yourself which preconceived goals and ambitions are important enough to hold onto and which should be altered or forgotten.

Few other situations occurring within the framework of marriage exert more strain upon the husband-wife relationship and yet, when respect and understanding grow accepting a handicapped child can provide deep compassion to strengthen the bonds of love into a truly satisfying and strong marriage.

Your responsibility as the parent of a handicapped child is great, but don't be afraid. This road to acceptance is not an unchartered path; many other parents have followed it (nearly 470,000 children in the United States are handicapped by cerebral palsy, for example). Nor is it a lonely path, for there are many other who will join you (each year about 250,000 babies are born in the United States with birth defects). There are known and predicted obstacles along the way, and although some of these can be real stumbling blocks, we live in an enlightened age and much has been learned about how these obstacles can be surmounted. Also, much has been discovered about the causes of deficiencies and about the methods by which handicapped children can best be trained to use the abilities they do have.

Equally important, just as the child has not been forgotten, neither have the parents been neglected, and there will be help for you along the way. Sometimes this help will be offered before you realize you need assistance, but most of the time you must let your needs be known. So, when you feel that you need help, don't hesitate to find someone qualified to help you! At times, just by talking with other parents whose children are also handicapped, you will gain an insight into the solution to your problem. At other times, and with different problems, you will benefit more from the aid and counsel of those people trained in the professions of treating personal problems. And, there are times when the father must lead the mother toward a helping hand, or the mother must realize that the father needs more help than she is able to give him.

Psychologists, counselors, and others who work with parents whose children are handicapped, have learned that there are certain milestones of emotional reactions along this road to acceptance. While the degree of intensity of reaction varies with different personalities and different types of handicapping deficiencies, and each stage overlaps others and reoccurs, the sequence that parents follow in learning to accept their child and his handicap is this: grief, denial, guilt, hostility, withdrawal, and rejection.

As each of these milestones is discussed in the following chapters, you will gain an insight into the reasons behind your emotions. You will also learn that other parents of handicapped children go through the same mental anguish and emotional turmoil as you experience, and often just knowing that you are "normal" helps to relieve some of the problem. Understanding this and learning ways in which others have found to overcome the situation will help you in making a good adjustment to this changed pattern of your life.

1. Grief

GRIEF IS THE FIRST milestone you will meet on the road to acceptance, your first emotional reaction to the fact that your child has such a deficiency in ability that he will be considered handicapped. This is a painful time for parents, but there is no detour around grief — nor should an effort be made to by-pass this stage, for it is a necessary and useful reaction. Grief is a transition period when the old dreams and expectations and anticipations are laid to rest so that preparation can then be begun for the new attitudes and a readjusted life pattern. Regardless of the child's age, the type or the degree of severity of the deficiency, all parents feel some form of grief when they first learn that their child is disabled.

But, while grief is useful and expected, it can be either a milestone or a stumbling block — which is up to you. You can revel in your self-imposed pity from now on and never progress past this preliminary stage; or, you can come to grips with your sorrow and go forward to meet life on its own terms. Fortunately, those other parents of handicapped children who have gone before you have left guideposts which will direct you toward the better path.

Acceptance is often thought of as being a passive, giving-into state of mind, but when parents are striving to learn how to admit that their child has a handicap, acceptance becomes active. It then is that state of mind in which conscious effort is made to recognize, understand, and resolve the problems. So, to be able to make the period of grief less painful and a positive and useful time, it is well to understand just what the emotion is. No two people react in the same way, each one has his own way of grieving, but knowing more about the emotion will help you have a clearer understanding of what it means in your particular situation.

First, what does the word itself mean? The *World Book Dictionary* defines grief as: "a deep sadness caused by trouble or loss"; *The American Heritage Dictionary* definition is: "intense mental anguish; deep remorse (the word anguish is defined as: "an agonizing or mental pain; torment, torture, suffering"). *Webster's New World Dictionary of the American Language* describes grief as: intense emotional suffering caused by loss, disaster, etc.; deep sorrow." Grief, therefore, is a sadness born out of a realization of loss. In your particular instance, it is a loss of the joys, dreams, and plans that you had anticipated through the expected normal progression of your child's growth and development.

Grief is a personal and a self-concerned feeling. There is no reason for you to feel ashamed because your first thoughts were centered on what the loss means to you personally, for that is the very nature of this particular emotion. Look back at the definitions — in every one the words used depict pain, and pain is personal. Now let me assure you, you've merited that anguish and despair you are suffering, for you have truly had a great loss. It is right that you should express your grief by mourning, so go ahead and cry. Weep if you can for there is a purpose in tears; tears cleanse the soul and make it possible for the mind to move ahead from that first state of shock and disbelief to the state of awareness of the disappointment.

It is disappointment that is at the basis of your grief and causes you to mourn — your disappointment that your child will not be what you had expected and hoped for. It is a deep disappointment which cuts to the very core of your sensitivity, but more than that, it is a shock so great that the very foundations of your life are threatened.

Whether the child's handicapping condition is known soon

after birth, or whether it is caused by an illness or accident later in life, or if it has become apparent over a period of several years, the parents still experience a feeling akin to numbness when the news is first "broken" to them. Sensing without really knowing yet what a tragedy this can turn out to be, there is that feeling of disbelief: "No, this cannot be happening to me!" For a time each parent feels wrapped up in his own transparent cocoon, isolated from the world of reality, and unconscious of his contact with other people. "I can't even remember driving home from the doctor's office" is a common reflection. Yet, at the same time, while the mind is trying to rebel against the truth, something deep inside knows that it *is* true and very real.

After the initial shock has begun to subside, the parents quite naturally continue to mourn their loss, but the first painful stage of grief cannot be allowed to continue. The tears have served the intended purpose of making the transition easier, and the parents must learn how to overcome their disappointment — or, at the very least, how to function in spite of their loss. Do not think for a moment that you will not experience other periods of grief and deep disappointment in the future as new situations develop, for you will. But now, in the beginning, is the time to lay the foundations of your method of attack against the depression of spirits which will inevitably follow. If you learn now how to handle your reactions, the grief periods will occur less frequently and will become less intense.

Because there is no way to look into the future and know the extent of the effect of the loss of ability, disappointment arising from a child's handicap is not a one-time thing; there is no definite ending to grief and disappointment — only an ending to the particular circumstance that illustrates the child's inability to perform as other children do. But just as there is no end to disappointment, so is there no end to hope, only an altering of the goals that you hope your child will reach.

We have seen that a feeling of grief, of mourning over the

loss of the anticipated "perfect child" is a natural and human way to feel, but what can be done to change this self-concerned state of mind? Parents cannot continue to live under this dark gloom. First, thoughts have to be turned away from self and toward someone else and his needs. I can give to you no magic formula, no secret. The only way is to make a conscious effort to think less of your own feelings and more about others. You begin to think constructively, to resist being blown about by the whims of your emotions. The time for self-pity is over, for while pity of self is natural it can only destroy when allowed to continue. There is no place for pity in the growing and maturing you must do in order to rise above your troubles. If, that is, you want to conquer the situation rather than let yourself be conquered by it.

Each Child Has Two Parents

The first person to consider should be the other parent — your husband or wife. Right now, at the very beginning of your life as parents of a child who is handicapped, you two must make up your minds whether you are going to be a team working together, or if you are going to let this tragedy break you apart. Achieving togetherness as a team requires effort on the part of each parent. Care only about how you feel and this will be the wedge that separates you two. If both of you consciously strive to help each other overcome the difficult times, you will find that you are in closer communion, have deeper and stronger love ties, and a marriage that transcends heights which you never dreamed possible. Edgar A. Guest begins his poem "Home" with the words "It takes a heap o' living in a house to make it home," and believe me, it takes a heap o' effort to fight this assault against your love for each other and against your marriage. However, you will find that once you've set the pattern of working together and being concerned for each other, this attitude will become such a part of your personality that you cannot function otherwise. Togetherness becomes a way of living for you both, and a way of loving.

So how do you begin? You begin by consoling each other, by realizing that the other one is also hurting and crying. You had dreams and anticipations, so did your wife or husband. His, too, were destroyed by the words that gave definition to your child's problems. Make the effort to understand by putting yourself in the other one's shoes; then you will find the words and gestures to show each other that you do understand. Eventually you will realize that the other one's reaction is directed toward the situation itself and not toward you personally. For example, a wife must understand that her husband's desire for aloneness is his way of trying to work out his own reactions and answers, not a rejection of her presence. So, also, his desire to return to the involvement of his work is not "running away from" the home and problems, but a real need to find some balance between what he can successfully do and has control over and what he feels he has failed to do and cannot control. His silence and reluctance to talk about the handicap may not be a refusal to admit the reality, but the only manner by which he can manage to control his emotions. Understand that your husband has his own way of showing grief and his own ways of combating the fears that the prospect of his responsibilities and obligations arouse in him.

Husbands, you must also make the effort to understand your wife's feelings and reactions. Her involvement right now with your child does not mean she cares less for you, but that her sense of motherhood is coming first right now, because she knows that her child needs her love and care and concern more than you need her. Understand, too, that she has been hit just as hard by this tragedy as you have been. In fact, in many aspects, she has been hit harder. You have a chance to forget, for a while at least, but she is with your child all day long with little or nothing to distract her thoughts from her loss and her sense of failure. (Even if your wife has a job outside the home, there is always a part of her mind that cannot forget, because she is a woman and that is part of being a mother.) The mother's contact with other people is usually confined to other mothers, and so she is constantly being reminded of the joys and pleasure she will be denied because her child will not be as other children are. Understand that her apathy toward you is not a rejection of you or even a withdrawal from you, but rather a result of her efforts to adjust her life and her thinking to this new turn her life has taken. Even her rejection of your love advances is basically not a rejection of you; she may be just physically tired. Certainly she is often depressed, and how can a woman feel loving and sexually aroused when she feels that she is less of a woman because she has produced a defective child, or because she has allowed her child to succumb to illness, or let him have an accident? You may think "that's just being a woman" and dismiss her feelings as being of little or no importance. Perhaps she *is* being "just a woman," but that makes it no less real in truth, because that is exactly how a woman does feel. Understand that your wife feels as she does for very valid and substantial reasons. If she cannot fight through her insecurity as a woman, she cannot express her love for you by being a woman.

When all is said and done, you will find love is the basis of your marriage, just as would be true if this had not happened to your child. Your love for each other will be the tie that will hold you together, and help you understand each other, and make each of you strong. Love is an out-going feeling, and the strange aspect of love is that the more one gives love, the more love one receives in return. Held in and not expressed, love dies because this emotion must be sent out and directed toward someone else. Tell each other of your love. Prove your love by the way you act, by your kindness toward one another, and by respect.

Showing respect means that you have faith in the other one's abilities, in the other one's strength of will power, talents, and capability to meet and solve the problems. But don't just *think* about respect, communicate! Talk about how you feel, encourage each other, use words to define those qualities in each other's personality you admire, the strength you recognize. Help each other put down and bury the seeds of fear and lack of confidence. Wives, tell your husband that he is no less capable or intelligent just because his son is mentally retarded. Husbands, tell your wife that she is no less a fully endowed woman just because, through some accident, the child she bore is deficient.

You two dreamed together and shared your hopes before this happened, did you not? So continue to dream and hope now. Your child's being handicapped has altered the paths you would have chosen to reach your goals, even altered the goals themselves in some instances, but that does not mean that you should not still have dreams to dream and hopes and aspirations to work toward.

Right now, you both feel that there can be little joy and pleasure to be found in your lives. Ahead, you can see only a dismal future, unrewarding and depressing. But that does not have to be so at all! Your joys and pleasures may be different from those of your friends, but they will be no less satisfying and enjoyable — unless you make them so. Help each other find the joy that life still has to offer; help each other laugh and to live each day to the fullest. You know, if each of you supports the other, *no* wind of adversity will be strong enough to blow either of you down.

Learning to give of yourself is important, but do not forget how to receive as well. Accepting words of love and praise is just as much a way of loving as is giving. But just accepting is not enough, you must let the giver know that you understand, believe, and appreciate those gifts of love. So husbands, when you come home from work to find that your wife has prepared a special meal, or even a time-consuming dish which you particularly like, recognize that as her gift of love and tell her so.

Or, wives, when your husband offers to baby-sit so that you can go out alone to shop or visit, recognize this as a gift of love from him and let him know that you understand and appreciate his thoughtfulness. (These are just "beginning thoughts," and the chapters "Wives" and "Husbands" include much more discussion about the various aspects of the husband-wife relationship.)

Don't Forget Your Child

But what about your child, the cause of all your grief?

The very first attitude you must change is believing that your child is the cause of your grief. He is not. Your grief is caused by the fact that your child has a handicapping deficiency in ability. Your child is still a child, he is only the innocent recipient of the results of whatever happened. If your child is an infant, he still has all the needs any baby has — to be fed and taken care of, to be played with, and to be loved. If he is an older child, he needs you even more than he did before the accident or illness, or as much as he did before you learned that he is deficient in ability and will be considered "handicapped." If the handicap is caused by illness or accident, he still must face the period of recuperation, and your showing him that your love is not altered or lessened will help him help himself. If he is healthy and strong physically, and you have received confirmation of your doubts and fears that "something is wrong," he still looks to you to satisfy the same needs today that he had yesterday. And the greatest of these needs is love.

Look beneath the handicap and see the child inside. Grieve not for his lack, but look for what he has. If he is an older child, he must now face making his own adjustment to his handicap. Certainly he must believe the reality of his handicap, but he also must believe that his life can continue in spite of what has happened. Your heart aches for him — for what he has lost, as well as for the mountain of problems he now must overcome.

Yet, you cannot grieve for him. Understand how he must feel, yes, but no pity or you'll weaken him and lessen his chances of rising above his adversity. One of the responsibilities of parenthood is helping the child develop what is good and strong within himself. This responsibility has not changed for you now, it has only become more important. If you pity him and let him know that you do, your child will never find the necessary strength he will need. Children tend to follow their parents' lead, and if you can learn to put aside your mourning and to appreciate every day's goodness, so will your child learn that there is good and pleasure to be found in his life.

Some parents, most often mothers, never progress beyond the stage of grief. Continually bemoaning this catastrophe which has befallen them, they are unable to look beyond the darkness of despair and despondency. And what a waste of lives it is when that happens — the child's life, as well as the mother's. The child may be refused the benefits of training, for example, because his mother believes there is no use since he is mentally retarded; the benefits of therapy are denied him because "poor Johnny's legs are crippled." Bosh! Perhaps Johnny will never be able to walk alone, but could he not be taught to use crutches or a wheelchair? Perhaps the child's intelligence is too low for him to be self-supporting and independent, but how can one know for sure until reasonable effort has been made to expand and develop the mind? Even when children are severely mentally retarded, the more they learn to do for themselves, the happier they are. There are many jobs which severely mentally handicapped people can be taught to perform that will give them a sense of usefulness and the feeling that life holds some purpose for them.

Consider the Grandparents

There are others who are concerned about this situation and who also grieve because of the loss — the grandparents. They, too, mourn; for not only do they love the particular parent who is their own child, but also the child who is a further extension of themselves. Yet, because they are seldom involved with the immediate situation, they find it difficult to learn the facts that would provide a foundation upon which they could base their understanding and acceptance.

Don't shut them out; keep them informed of what is happening and what is going on within your family. They will grieve anyway, so help them overcome their mourning by showing them that hope is obtainable. Don't use them just as a soft shoulder to cry upon — that is useful, but don't overdo your weeping with them. Try to explain the situation with the least coloring of doom and hopelessness, while still being careful not to gloss over the true facts. Sure, it is a hard balance to keep, and only by carefully listening to what they say, by reading their gestures to determine what they are feeling but not saying, can you hope to strike that careful balance. Even though you try to do the best you think possible and talk to and act toward them in the most deeply loving and kind manner, there will be times when you will be completely misunderstood. Because of that unique relationship between child and parent which carries over into the child's adult life, sensitivity and hidden emotions often combine to work against understanding. Try to keep in mind that despite your adult age, you are still your parents' child.

One approach that is positive and often shows results, but is very hard for children to follow, is to let the grandparents know that they are needed by the young parents — that they're not being "put out to pasture" or considered incapable of helping. There are many ways in which the grandparents can be very much needed; this situation is not short-term, it will last a long time and perhaps forever in your child's life. So, as with each other, you parents are going to have to find a way to build a good foundation of understanding between yourselves and your in-laws and your own parents. Believe me, all the effort you exert will be worthwhile, for you can find no better friends, no more loving and contributing helpers, than the grandparents.

Now, realistically, you'll have to face the fact that at times they will blame you, particularly if you are the in-law. They will never think that you are doing enough; or else, that you are devoting *too* much time and effort to your child. But, when you realize that often they must form their opinions in ignorance of the true situation because you've not given them the information, then you can take the proper steps toward correcting the misunderstanding and improving the quality of their feelings.

You must realize, too, that sometimes grandparents refuse to see the child or find all sorts of excuses for not doing so because they are afraid. They are afraid to accept the reality; they are afraid that they will say the wrong things and afraid that they will do something that will upset you even more. The quality of your relationship with your parents and your in-laws will depend to a great extent upon how well you are able to look at the situation from their viewpoint. You must realize, too, that their actions and words frequently are determined by their reaction to the handicap and are not directed toward you at all.

What does all this discussion have to do with grief? A great deal, because it is during the time of your mourning when these problems begin. If your relationship with the grandparents is good, then you will find them to be among your strongest allies and best of friends. Much of the responsibility for making this relationship a good one rests upon your shoulders.

Parting Thoughts About Grief

Grief is a natural and expected way for parents to feel when they learn that their child has some deficiency in ability that will classify him as "handicapped." To mourn is necessary, for it is the loss of the parents' dreams, anticipations, and expectations for their future with their child.

Since grief is a personal, self-concerned emotion, the tears shed during this time are beneficial because they help in washing away the old ideas and preparing the person to accept new attitudes. But, the grieving and the mourning must be consciously stopped, because just as with any other type of loss, life must go on and plans for the future must be considered.

How the parents handle this first emotional reaction does much to determine the pattern of their relationship with each other. By learning to forget self and by focusing attention on the other parent, a foundation of understanding is built. Through love and respect and the acceptance of each one's efforts to express love, their minds and sensitivities are tuned into the other's needs. By learning to work together to solve their problems, parents can build a good and meaningful relationship that will strengthen the bonds of their marriage and enable both of them to reach heights of achievement and a depth of love never dreamed possible before.

So shed those tears; then wipe them away. Stop moaning about what you have lost — you have no idea of what you can gain. All is not lost; tomorrow is a new day and there is much to be done and enjoyed. You can survive even this catastrophe; others have. Are you any less capable than hundreds of thousands of other parents?

2. Denial

THE TIME COMES when the initial shock subsides, the sharp pangs of grief are dulled, there are no more tears left to shed, and the parents begin to realize the enormity of the consequences of their child's handicap. Now they find themselves denying that there is something wrong with their child, or else refusing to believe that the condition will be permanent and that there is no known cure.

Being unwilling to admit that your child has a lack of ability which will be a handicap to him in the future is a perfectly normal and human reaction. Goodness knows, no parent wants to admit that his child is anything less than perfect, and to have to face the fact of a final, unalterable deficiency in ability seems to be the same as giving up hope that the future will be anything but dismal and without purpose or pleasure. Denial is a basic human reaction toward an unpleasant fact. Somehow, we think, by refusing to recognize that this is real, it will not be. Denial is a defense against the onslaught of whatever force is threatening the sense of security, but it is a defense mechanism which can be both useless and destructive.

Useless because refusing to accept the reality of your child's handicap certainly will not make the problems disappear. Destructive because you will actually be harming your child's chances for happiness by impeding his own acceptance of his limitations and by making it impossible for him to learn through special training and therapy how to make the most of the abilities he does have.

Fear Lies behind Denial

Fear is a major part of the reason why parents fight so hard against admitting that their child has a handicap, and there are good and very valid causes for their fear: the uncertainty of the future because so few guidelines can be given for the child's potentiality; the doubts that they will be able to meet the responsibilities demanded by the handicap; the overriding and unanswerable question "What will happen to him?" gives rise to a sense of fear that at times is close to panic.

This sense of panic is different from that which most people experience at one time or another in their lives, for this is a circumstance to which there is no end, an enigma to which there is no ready solution. Rather, it seems to be only a prelude to a series of unsolvable problems, of challenges and responsibilities which demand more ability and strength than the parents feel they possess. Still, incapable as they feel themselves to be, each parent knows instinctively that somewhere the strength must be found to conquer this awesome and almost overpowering fear — and the easiest way is not recognizing the reality of the handicapping condition.

You parents who are still fighting against fear (and most of us do, you know), consider this: this fear, this heart-constricting sense of panic from which you are trying to escape, is caused by an emotional reaction to the unknown. As you contemplate the future, you feel as if you are beginning a journey across an uncharted wasteland with no one to guide your steps. But you *do* have guides, and again there are examples to follow which will help you chart your own way. You are not the first to have a child with this particular handicap, and help is available for you from many different sources — the advice of other parents who have had similar experiences and the constant advancement of research in the fields of psychology, medicine, and education that increases the knowledge of those people who are trained in ways to treat and educate your child and to counsel you. (For further examples, see the chapter "Sources of Help.")

Certainly you have a gigantic challenge to face — many unusual challenges, in fact — but you cannot make these challenges disappear by running away and pretending that the condition does not exist.

But wait just a minute. No one asks you to meet all these parent to a handicapped child must take a tremendous amount of strength of character, and I am just not that strong. Besides, how will I know the right things to do? Suppose I make mistakes?" (In addition, fathers have their own particular set of fear-causing worries such as, "Where will I ever get all the money we'll need?")

But wait just a minute. No one asks you to meet all these challenges at once, or to solve all the problems today. Because you are only human, you will make mistakes with your child — there has never been a parent who hasn't. Strength of character is not an inborn quality, but one which is learned through the process of living. Don't try to anticipate problems that don't yet exist, for much of what you fear now will never come about. The time will come when you will need to make some long-range plans for the future, but right now, you need to solve only today's problems today.

If you look at the long-distance scope of the situation, you will be overwhelmed by the mountain of problems. Just as walking begins by taking one step at a time, your first step now is to take a hard look at the evidence and then to admit that your child has a deficiency in ability — in other words, that your child is "handicapped." Only then will you begin to conquer your fear. With this victory, you can begin to take the second step toward constructive action.

The Frustrating Unknowns

One of the aspects of this entire situation hardest to adjust to is the frustration that arises from the lack of definite information.

There is little wonder that parents who are trying to understand and accept their child's handicap often have the feeling that they are fighting an unknown assailant in the dark. Every specialist to whom they turn seems to have a different opinion of the cause and a different solution to their child's problems.

When you find yourself becoming frustrated and not knowing which way to turn, when you become angry because doctors and others will not give you definite answers to your questions, remember that they cannot because there is no possible way to know the answers. Many types of handicaps are difficult to diagnose in the earlier stages, especially when the child is very young. With other handicapping conditions, only through observation of development or recuperation over a period of as much as several years, can an assessment of ability be made. The doctors cannot tell you whether your child will walk or not, because they cannot measure individual rate of healing; they cannot tell you how long it will be before your child can read, or even perhaps whether he *will* read, because they cannot measure the rate of your child's development that closely.

WARNING: Do not succumb to the temptation of letting the disagreeing opinions overcome your recognition of the reality of the existence of the handicapping condition. Think back to what was actually said, not to what you want to remember. Be sure that you are not grasping at straws to build your wall of denial. Rather than using the differing opinions as a basis for convincing yourself that your child has no deficiency, let the evidence you've been given guide your thinking toward accepting the limitations of his ability.

The Father's Denial

According to the results of a study of families of handicapped children (Harold D. Love. *Parental Attitudes Toward Exceptional Children.* Springfield, Illinois: Charles C. Thomas, 1970), the father's attitude toward the child and toward his handicap sets the pattern for the attitudes of the entire family. When he admits that the handicap exists and accepts the child with his limitations, so does the family; when he denies that the child has a handicap and rejects the child because of his lack of ability, the family members tend to follow his lead, especially the brothers and sisters. (You see, fathers, here is proof that you are more important to your family than perhaps you thought you were.)

There are many reasons which may lie behind a father's difficulty in accepting the truth of his child's handicap, but the one contributing factor I have observed most often is the lack of information. Because it is usually the mother who takes the child to the doctors, and she with whom the teachers discuss the child's progress (or lack of progress), the father is left to rely upon secondhand, filtered information. He seldom has the opportunity to talk over his doubts, his fears, or his observations with someone who can enlighten his understanding.

I am afraid that much of the blame for not knowing must be placed upon the fathers themselves. The doctor can ask the father to "come in for a talk," the teachers can request the father's presence at a conference, the mother can suggest that he go with her to the child's appointment with a specialist, but there is no force strong enough to make him go. His wife can try to discuss the situation with him, but she cannot make him listen.

Some fathers simply do not want to know. "Raising the kids is a wife's job," they say. "I've got all I can handle trying to provide for them." Nonaction by other fathers is due to their fear that their doubts will be substantiated. When no evidence proving otherwise is known, they can keep their heads in the sand and pretend to see development and improvement when there is none.

This attempt to hide from the reality is seldom a conscious effort, especially at the beginning. But fathers have other responsibilities on which they must concentrate, and mothers are usually much more involved with child care. Because a father spends less time with his handicapped child, he has less opportunity to notice problems, and it is easier for him to over-look any evident problems in favor of others which seem to be more pressingly urgent.

But eventually the day arrives when the truth can no longer be concealed. When that inevitable time comes and the reality of the situation hits, the impact may be too much for the un-prepared father to accept and handle in a reasonable and re-sponsible manner. Learning to admit that one of our children is handicapped by some deficiency, either mental or physical, is a painful and difficult process, but the pain is easier to bear when realization comes gradually. When the truth is taken in small doses, it can be absorbed on a day-by-day basis, and a parent has a chance to build up his strength so that acceptance of the finality of the handicapping condition is but another step in a long series of readjustments.

Think, too, of how much harder the mother's task is when the father does not admit that their child is handicapped. She must then bear the burden of responsibility alone, and her share is heavy enough.

Finally, by not admitting the reality of the handicap, fathers deny themselves the help and counsel which could make their adjustment easier. How can a counselor guide a father through the intricacies of understanding his child's problems, lead him in making good decisions for the family and for the child, when the father does not admit that his child is handicapped?

Mothers Deny the Handicap Too

Every mother who has a handicapped child finds herself torn between two principal states of mind — the instinctive realiza-tion that "something is wrong" and the overwhelming, protec-tive instinct to prove that the cause is to be found in some out-side force rather than being a manifestation of some lack within the child. In other words, rationalization — the same attitude as excuse-finding and just as unrealistic and potentially damaging.

To face the fact that this deviation from the norm is caused by a nonreversible, permanent condition is, at the beginning, beyond the ability of most mothers. Because deep down in the mind of each mother lurks the fear that admitting to the truth of a child's slow development or poor performance would exemplify her lack of ability to be a good mother, it is a natural and human instinct to resist evidence that would substantiate the reality of the child's handicapping deficiency. With this attitude governing her thinking, the mother whose child has a handicap sees ability and development that do not exist, and she puts blinders on so that she can better conceal the obvious even from herself.

Although it may seem to be the easier way, this turning away from the truth cannot be continued. Denying the presence of a problem never leads to the solution; to apply the philosophy of "ignore it and it will go away" is immature and irresponsible. Actually, it is as if you were denying the existence of your child himself, for the handicap is a part of him. You love your child with his handicap, not despite his lack of ability, or in spite of his short-comings.

Parental Denial Affects the Child

What is happening to the child while his parents are going to all this effort to prove that he is not really different — that he is not mentally retarded, or crippled, or blind, or deaf, or emotionally unstable? How is he being affected by his parents' attitude?

First, he is being denied the love of his parents. Their fight against accepting his inability to measure up to their standards obscures their natural and spontaneous love for their child. In loving another person one must accept that person as he is with all his faults and inabilities, because these characteristics are an integral part of the personality. This concept of love is no less true when considering our own children. In line with these thoughts of love, by denying the existence of the handicap, the parents also are responsible for the destruction of the child's very necessary sense of security that is built through his knowledge that he is a source of pleasure and happiness to his parents — that they are happy because he is their child. Although the problems caused by the handicap can seem to obscure any pleasure that the child may be capable of bringing to his parents, every child possesses some source of joy for his parents.

On a more practical and objective line of thought, the child suffers because he is denied the treatment and education that would enable him to make the most of his remaining abilities. In most types of handicaps the younger the child is when a program of therapy and training is begun, the greater will be his progress in his development. Also, the sooner the child becomes acquainted with the use of braces, crutches, hearing aids, wheelchairs, or prosthetic devices, the easier it will be for him to accept this as a part of himself, and the better his adjustment to his differentness will be.

Consider the effect upon the child of the unrealistically high level of achievement that his parents may set for him because they cannot admit his lack of ability. His self-esteem suffers, and he becomes convinced that he is a failure simply because he cannot match his performance and ability to his expectations, which have been set by his parents. A child who is handicapped has to suffer enough blows to his concept of self-worth — he doesn't need more from his parents.

Children often feel that they are the cause of their parents' unhappiness. With a handicapped child, especially one who is not extremely mentally retarded, this natural tendency may become so frequent that it becomes an obsession, resulting in suicidal thoughts and even in attempts to take his own life.

While these instances are extremes, it is certainly not hard to understand how such a situation arises when a handicapped child feels that because he is such a disappointment to his parents and such an instrument of their torment, that those whom he loves would be happier if he were dead. You see, you are playing with fire, and the consequences can be equally destructive when allowed to get out of control.

The Grandparents

The grandparents are more prone to deny the existence and the finality of the child's handicap than are the parents. While their attitudes and their acceptance are not as important to the child as the feelings of his parents, the grandparents often play a very important role in the life of the child and his family, because their feelings and attitudes are important to the child's parents.

Many of the obstacles which impede the grandparents' understanding and acceptance of the child's handicap are similar to those which the parents meet. Just as knowledge helps the parents understand and accept the child and his handicap, so is knowledge important and necessary in helping the grandparents. Do keep your parents informed (you'll be surprised at how smart they are, and how quickly they may grasp the situation). Don't keep them completely in the dark, but let them know the results of the tests, and the opinions of the doctors and teachers and therapists. Tell them what the specialists have told you about the possibilities for improvement and development and the recommended program of therapy and training. In answering their questions, you will often find that you are also answering your own and, in the process, gaining a clearer insight into your own feelings.

Let the grandparents know what your child's limitations as well as his abilities are, but don't paint a picture that is entirely dark and dismal. Remember that he is important to them, too. They love this child, and they, too, are beset with fears for his future. They also suffer heartbreak because this has happened.

At times you will have to convince the grandparents that you are following the best course of action, according to your own understanding and resources. You will learn that at times you will have to reassure them that the team of teachers, doctors, therapists, and psychologists to whom you look for advice and counsel are quite capable, and that since you trust their decisions, they must in turn trust you to do what is best for their grandchild.

Above all, don't try to conceal from them the cause of the handicap, but let them know the truth as you understand it. (Of course, there are circumstances when you may find it best to spare them some of the details.) Most of the time when in-laws blame the incidence on the other side of the family, it is because they lack the knowledge that would lead to their understanding. Being sure that they have this knowledge is your responsibility.

Remember, too, that if your family is typical of the average American family of this day and age, you do not live close to either set of grandparents, so they do not have much opportunity to observe your child. If this fits your situation, remember that they are dependent upon you to keep them informed and to give them as accurate a picture as you can.

Searching for the Rainbow's End — The Cure

Denial can be expressed by passively turning away and ignoring the existence of the handicapping deficiency, but there is another form of denial which can be even more destructive and dangerous — fighting against accepting the finality of the damage which makes the handicap a permanent condition. It is this attitude that so often leads parents on a fruitless search for the impossible-to-find cure. It can be a search as unrealistic as the search for the pot of gold at the end of the rainbow, the only rewards being broken dreams and shattered hopes and unhappiness for both the parents and their child.

I speak in strong language about this because I've known parents who have wasted their time and money, sacrificing their own lives as well as their child's, in the belief that somewhere there must be someone who can offer a complete cure. Now this is a far different kind of searching than that of trying to find someone who can determine the cause of the problems, or searching for someone who knows how to treat this particular condition, because then the search is for answers and guidance as to what to do, rather than for a miraculous cure to the known problem.

"But I can't live without hope," you are saying. Of course you can't, but let your hope be realistic. Instead of chasing from one doctor to another to find the one who will agree that your child's condition is something he will "grow out of" or one who promises a "sure cure," concentrate on helping your child learn how to develop the ability that he has and finding ways in which he can compensate for his handicap. For instance, if your child is blind, don't look for some cure when reputable and responsible physicians have determined that the damage is irreparable. Instead, find the type of education and training that can teach him to read braille and use his skills to become independent. Or, if your child is mentally retarded, don't look for the magic that will lift the veil from his bound-in intelligence — provide the schooling and training that will unlock his ability as it is so that he can make the most of what he is capable of doing.

The parents who slip most easily into the pitfalls of both denial of the handicap and of rainbow-chasing for the cure are those whose children's handicaps are relatively minor. They have so few guidelines to follow because so few definite conclusions can be drawn. The child who is classified as a "slow learner" may have a slight brain damage (now frequently expressed by the term "minimally brain-damaged") that affects only one area of his learning so that he learns to read, but cannot grasp the concepts of math, or he may simply lack motivation, or his "slowness" may include all areas of his learning ability. Because minor deficiencies are often so hard to detect and even harder to label, it may be years before the real cause of the problems is determined and even longer before corrective treatment begins to show results. Even after the cause of the difficulty is learned, the parents may still wonder if the corrective measures they are following are the best — or if they are on the right track at all.

The inescapable burden which parents whose children are minimally handicapped bear is "Have I done enough?" They wonder, "Would a little more therapy, another medication, another kind of treatment, make him normal? Did I stop too soon, or was the answer just around the corner?"

One of the hardest decisions which parents of all handicapped children have to make is when to stop looking for a cure. While this may seem to imply giving up and loss of hope, it isn't at all. Rather, it is a realistic attitude. Released from the pressure of leaving no stone unturned, of thinking there might be hiding the one way in which the child will be made "normal," the parents are then free to make decisions and plans that are more realistic and in the best interest of the child.

3. Guilt

OF ALL THE STUMBLING BLOCKS on a parent's road to acceptance, the one of guilt is perhaps the most formidable, for unresolved, guilt can undermine the progress that has been made toward accepting the reality of the handicap and make constructive action toward adjustment impossible.

Guilt, and the causes of guilt, tends to follow a similar pattern for all parents whose children are handicapped. However, because we are all individuals, each of us has different deeds that make us feel guilty, just as we experience varying degrees of intensity of the guilt-remorse emotion.

All parents must assume the responsibility at times for what happens to their children, and all parents have reason to blame themselves for having made unwise decisions or taken wrong action concerning their children. But when a child is handicapped, his parents feel more accountable for what happened to him, and the self-blame they feel is more intense because of the enormity of the consequences and the damage that often cannot be rectified.

In the following discussion the term "guilt-imp" is used to refer to particular misdoings (deeds or decisions) which parents may feel caused their child's handicap and for which they blame themselves. Guilt is a very personal feeling, and yet to be resolved the cause must be considered objectively and analyzed in as clear logic as possible. Learning to think of guilt as being caused by those "small demons" of self-blaming thoughts helps to depersonalize responsibility, thereby lessening self-condemnation so that one's guilt can then be resolved.

Before we go on to look at guilt more closely, again an understanding of the meaning of the word itself may prove to be helpful. In *The American Heritage Dictionary* guilt is defined as: "the fact of being responsible for a wrong-doing; remorseful awareness of having done something wrong." (And remorse is defined as: "moral anguish arising from repentance for past misdeeds; bitter regret." The word is derived from a Latin word meaning "biting back" or "to bite again." And how our remorse can "bite" again and again.) There is a shade of difference in the *World Book Dictionary* definition: "having done something wrong, deserving to be blamed and punished." (And isn't that exactly the way we feel at times — that we *deserve* to be punished because of what we've done wrong? How often, if there is no one else to punish us, what a good job we can do of punishing ourselves!)

Now don't condemn all aspects of guilt as being wrong. Quite the contrary, for feelings of guilt or remorse provide one of the most necessary and effective restraints on human behavior. Without guilt, civilized society would retreat back into the jungle, for the ability to feel guilt distinguishes man from the animals. But guilt must be mastered, else it will master the person; the good of guilt can be — and must be — extracted and used as a tool for guidance and understanding.

"That's all well and good," you say, "but how do I do that?" Your first step is to learn to recognize the feeling for what it is. Guilt seldom arrives into our thinking unannounced; each guilt-imp usually emits the same alarm sound — the words "if only" followed by whatever past misdeed happens to be causing the remorse at the time. So, you learn to isolate the deed so that you are able to look at it objectively. Don't, don't, for heaven's sake, try to ignore your feelings of guilt. If you try to push the guilt-imps back into your mind behind conscious thought, they will only grow in strength, ready to attack you again. Repeated attacks on your conscience may lead to your defeat.

Many times the reasons for guilt and self-blame lie deep

within a parent's past, because the personality one develops determines what he feels guilty about, how he reacts to his guilt feelings, and the extent of his remorse. Therefore, this discussion can be only superficial. However, I hope you will find the guidance by which you can dispel some of your own particular guilt-imps. Do not expect to be strong enough or knowledgeable enough to handle all your guilt by yourself. Regardless of what you read, of how much you study, or even how much you know about human behavior, you still need the help of those people who are trained and experienced in counseling. You'll be surprised at how quickly such a person can steer you into the right paths of thought, and how much pain and suffering you will be spared. Talk to your doctor, your minister, to someone in the family counseling service in your town.

Guilt and the Birth Injury

At first, while you are still trying to overcome your grief, guilt-imps may strike from all sides. These will no doubt pertain to what you think to be the cause of the handicap, what you believe happened to cause the disabling injury. When the handicapping condition is recognized soon after birth, some of the more common guilt-imps that attack mothers are: "If only I'd quit smoking," "If only I'd stayed on that diet my doctor gave me," "If only I hadn't gone on that trip," "If only I'd not painted the nursery," "If only I'd called the doctor that time I felt so funny and my back hurt." For fathers, some of the more common guilt-imps are: "If only I'd helped her more around the house," "If only I'd not insisted on making love," "If only I had gotten her to the hospital sooner," "If only I'd paid more attention to her complaining about her aches and pains," "If only I'd made her stop working sooner."

These particular guilt-imps usually can be explained away by the doctors and by clear and logical thinking on your part. Tell your doctor about your doubts and your guilt feelings, for although he has probably heard all these before from other patients, he will not know just what yours are and will hesitate to mention any for fear that you've not thought about that particular one. He will not want to worry you any more than you are already. Don't feel ashamed of what you've done or not done, don't even let your disobedience to his instructions or orders stand in the way of your peace of mind. Your doctor is not your judge, he is your physician, and as such he is interested in the health of your mind as well as the health of your body. He will tell you, for example, that certainly heavy smoking by a pregnant woman is harmful to the unborn baby, but seldom does this fact in itself cause a serious birth defect. Simple overweight harms the mother more than the baby. Women have been known to have sustained serious accidents and still give birth to perfectly healthy babies. Healthy babies are born outside hospitals every day. Thousands of women are active in their jobs up to the very last of their pregnancies. Did you know that some doctors have advanced the theory that sexual intercourse during the last stages of labor has a beneficial effect on the mother and helps to make delivery easier for the baby? For almost every reason you can dredge up to blame yourself for what has happened, a dozen logical explanations can be found as to why you were not the cause. Even when you took medication that your doctor did not prescribe, or did not follow his orders, even if you became infected with some disease (yes, even venereal disease) which you passed on to your child, medical science has discovered how to counteract many of the effects. Much has been learned about handicaps that are caused by the genetic incompatability of the parents, and new knowledge of detection and prevention is constantly being gained. If you were unaware of this problem, how then can you be the cause of your child's resulting handicap?

Letting your guilt grow until you are controlled by your remorse and self-incrimination does no one any good at all. You cannot allow yourself to dwell on what you might have done that caused something to go wrong with your baby's development; or what you did not do that may have prevented the handicapping deficiency. Whatever happened has happened; the cause is all in the past now; it is done. Looking back in self-blame cannot alter the results. It can only serve to make you less able to handle the situation as it now is. You've a child to love, and that child needs your love. Guilt can be a barrier to the natural feelings of tenderness, concern, and love which you have and want to express toward your child. Because guilt can be the cause of so much pain, the person around whom the guilt is centered can become the object of not love, but hate — even an innocent baby.

As time passes and your child grows older, the guilt-imps will march under another banner: "Why am I being punished?" All sorts of past misdeeds are then revived to haunt your thoughts. One of the most persistently haunting misdeeds is premarital sex. Regardless of how "modern" we thought ourselves, how "right" it seemed to be at the time, the moralist teachings of our society tell us that this is wrong. So, it is therefore only natural that in the search for the reason why, often this becomes the logical wrong-doing that merited the punishment. Another guilt-imp that haunts many parents when a child is handicapped is the memory that this child was not wanted or planned at the beginning. The guilt-ridden mind can illogically and easily believe that because this baby was not really wanted, the handicap is a form of punishment for the parents. Or that the mother's negative thoughts had some ill effect upon the developing fetus. These are but two of many causes of the guilt-punishment syndrome.

If you believe your child's handicap is your punishment for wrong-doing or wrong-thinking, stop and look at your guilt-imps logically. Are you not condemning yourself because of your moral judgments based on the teachings of your religion? If you are, perhaps you have forgotten a very basic teaching — the concept that the Lord is a God of love. If that is so, and it must be, for this is one of the principles on which Christianity and the parent religion of Judaism are based, would He then punish an innocent child because of your actions or sins? Are you thinking now of: "And the sins of the fathers shall be visited upon their sons and their sons' sons"? (Exodus 34:7) If you will read that passage, you will discover that it concerns the sin of the lack of faith. For a lengthier discussion of this topic, turn to the chapter "Your Relationship with Your God."

Guilt and Accident or Illness

Parents whose children are handicapped because of an accident or illness have their own particular sort of hell to live through with guilt. Often their guilt-imps are more definite; cause and result more directly discernible.

These guilt-imps also herald their coming with "If only" — "If only I hadn't let Johnny go alone to the store," "If only I hadn't stopped to visit with Mrs. B. in the parking lot," "If only I'd gone to him when I first heard him cry out," "If only I'd taken her to the doctor sooner, instead of thinking it was just a bad cold," "If only I'd not kept putting off giving her the measles vaccine." Or, "If only we'd not let him have that motorcycle," "If only I had not gone back to work and had been home when he came in from school." Sure, perhaps you were responsible, but how many other parents do you know who have been guilty of the same negligence and no tragedy resulted? Or, for that matter, how many other times have you followed the same course of action, or inaction, and nothing happened?

Naturally you feel that you are responsible for what happened, whether it was an illness or an accident that led to the handicap. But you cannot continue to dwell on your part of the cause. You must find a way to resolve your feelings of guilt, or you'll find that you will be ineffective in coping with the situation now. How? You begin to lay your guilt to rest by realizing that no one knows just why tragedies occur. Accidents, whether they be man-caused or accidents of nature, happen without rhyme or reason. Whatever happened to cause injury to your child is done now; it is over. Now you must look toward the future, not back to the past. No amount of self-chastisement, no amount of questioning, nothing that you can do will undo what happened; you cannot turn back the clock. All of your searching for the reason why, your self-incrimination, your self-punishment take energy that you need and should be expending in more constructive action. You bet it's hard — oh, how I know — to put these thoughts behind you. But you have to forget. You must resolve those thoughts of having been responsible for your child's condition, otherwise the guilt-imps will grow until you will fall beneath the weight.

Consider this line of thought: even if you should discover the reason why this happened and learn that you were indeed the cause, would it really make any difference now? Would the consequences be altered? Would your child not be mentally retarded, or cerebral palsied? Would his legs not be lame, would his eyes see or his ears hear? Nothing would be changed, and you can accomplish no good at all by continuing to blame yourself for causing your child's handicap.

As long as you allow your thoughts to dwell on your guilt, your ability to think positively and to act constructively will be thwarted, for the two opposing attitudes cannot live together in the same mind. Stop for a minute and listen to your heart — you will hear the faint sounds of love and reason. Heed those sounds. Guilt is a negative emotion, and you need all the positives you can find.

Your Guilt and Your Child

Laying the guilt-imps to rest is important not only for the parents' peace of mind and adjustment, but also for the sake of the handicapped child. The parents not only suffer, their child is harmed when they are unable to resolve their guilt because any emotion that is so instrumental in setting the tone of the parents' attitudes also influences their feelings toward the child and tempers the way they treat him.

Although guilt is a natural and necessary human emotion, man must build up some sort of defense against it, or he cannot survive under the burden. The problem lies in finding the right kind of defensive counteraction that will be the most beneficial to all concerned. The key to success is the ability to distinguish between positive counteraction and that which will prove to be negative. This is far from being an easy task, but again there are other parents who have traveled the same route, and they have left you a guidebook.

It is the rare parent who has not looked at his handicapped child and thought, "If it were not for me, you would not be in this condition." The first instinct then is to try to "make it up to him" by denying him nothing that would bring even a small moment of joy and happiness into his life, and doing nothing that might cause him even a second of unhappiness. You many be thinking that this is an admirable way for parents to feel, but in truth, it is a negative defensive action because the parents' actions are motivated by their attempts to appease their own guilt-imps, and the handicap becomes more important than the child himself. Thus, the parents' feelings of guilt lead them to overindulge their child. When the child is an infant, overindulgence may be continuing to treat him as if he were a baby long after he has passed that need. It is a natural child reaction to resist growing up and learning, and so by continuing to treat the child as if he were as helpless as an infant, they are denying him the opportunity to use and develop the capabilities he has. Or, the older child is allowed to wallow in his self-pity — and even encouraged to do so — rather than being encouraged and helped to overcome and find compensations for his handicapping deficiency. Following this logic, the child's therapy may be discontinued because "the exercises hurt him so much," or his schooling may be stopped because "he doesn't like school." Even the rudiments of good discipline may not be taught, and so the child doesn't learn the principles of self-discipline.

"Ridiculous!" you say? Not at all. I've known just this kind of nonaction to be followed by parents who sincerely thought that they were doing the very best for their child.

Twenty-two-year-old Louise, for example, mentally retarded but not physically handicapped, who could have been taught self-care and simple skills which would have given her reason for self-respect and widened her interests was not, because her parents would not let her go to a special school. "She didn't like school, and we didn't have the heart to make her go. It's our place to look after her; it was our fault she's the way she is, you know." And so Louise sits hour after hour in her rocking chair, or swings aimlessly in her swing, never smiling, not making any attempt to enjoy life.

Or in the case of Johnny, whose legs were paralyzed as a result of a motorcycle accident. For ten years he has lain in his bed, except when his father comes home from work and carries him into the living room to watch television. The doctors told his parents there was a chance his legs could be repaired through surgery, but they refused. "We just couldn't let him go through all that pain; he'd been through so much already." Physical therapy and teaching Johnny to use braces, or at least a wheel-chair, had been recommended, and his parents refused to carry through. "All that training and the therapy would've been so hard on him and using those braces or the wheelchair was so embarrassing — he didn't even want to go out of the house. We decided to just make him happy ourselves. After all, it's our fault, we bought him that motorcycle."

Overprotecting the handicapped child usually goes hand in hand with overindulgence. Overcompensation is perhaps a good definitive word for both reactions. Wrapping a child who is handicapped in cotton wool by not letting him play with other children who are not handicapped because of fear that he will be hurt, not giving him the opportunity or encouragement to try to reach beyond his ability as they see it, only serves to make a handicapped child even more dependent upon his parents and less capable of achieving a sense of independence.

Many, many times handicapped children will be able to become participating and contributing adult members of society, if they are given the right kind of training. By shielding the child from contact with the outside world, his parents deny him the chance to learn how to take his place in the "normal" world and to cope with his adjustment to a world designed for nonhandicapped people.

There are other ways in which the effects of the parents' unresolved guilt can harm the child, and not the least of these is the fostering of a feeling of shame in the parents' attitude. Most often today shame is seen not as being ashamed of the child, but ashamed because the handicap exists. It is a reaction that can prevent the parents from admitting the full extent of the deficiency even to those to whom they've turned for help for their child. For example, a mentally deficient child may be entered in the regular public school classroom with no mention from his parents of his learning difficulties. By the time the teacher discovers his learning problems for herself, the child's self-esteem and sense of worth have already taken a beating, to say nothing of the time he has wasted. How much happier he would have been, and how much more he would have profited, had his parents admitted that his ability to learn is below the average and placed him in a special class where teaching methods would have been geared to his level of learning. In too many instances the doctors and therapists and teachers are hindered in their attempts to formulate an effective program for the child's training and treatment, because they are given a glorified picture of the child's accomplishments and rate of development.

Not only does unresolved guilt lead to overprotection of the child, it also can lead to parent-martyrdom — self-sacrifice and self-denial by the parents in order to meet the child's assumed needs. You may be thinking, "But what is so wrong with that?" Nothing, if this is not allowed to go to extremes. All good parents make sacrifices for their children, every parent denies himself things he wants and needs so that he can meet his child's needs and desires. That is part of love, and it is certainly an expression of parent-love and responsibility. But by giving up too much — the father, a satisfying career, the mother, her participation in her own activities, their social life, financial security — the handicapped child is harmed more than he is helped. Family harmony, so very important and necessary for the child who has a handicap, can be easily broken by resentment when the other children in the family are forced to sacrifice the fulfillment of their own needs in favor of the handicapped sibling. The guilt-imps are not dispelled through undue sacrifice and martyrdom, they only grow in strength to undermine the parent's ability to think positively. Eventually the resentment that has grown out of self-sacrifice overpowers the love the parents once felt for their child — and eventually, for each other.

Summary

The purpose of this discussion about guilt is not to frighten you, but rather to make you realize the important role that guilt plays in determining the quality of your acceptance and adjustment to the fact that your child has a handicapping deficiency of ability. To feel guilty because your child is not "normal" is only to be human, but you cannot simply let it go at that. You must resolve your guilt. And, since it is the very rare individual who can successfully accomplish this alone, you will need outside help. Fortunately this help is only as far away as your doctor, your minister or rabbi, and trained counselors such as psychologists and social workers. The guilt complex is a complicated emotion, and not one the sufferer is equipped to handle alone. Seek out a well-qualified, experienced counselor, for this is too important to trust to a casual amateur; nor is this a do-it-yourself project.

This book is not intended to take the place of professional counselors, only to augment their work and to help you gain the necessary self-confidence that you can only achieve through understanding and acceptance of yourself.

Being the parent of a handicapped child is a hard, demanding task, often confusing and frequently demoralizing. Still, underneath all the mental turmoil and emotional anguish, lie those instincts that will guide you in the right direction, if you only listen.

Because an unresolved sense of guilt can cause a wall to rise around your instinctive better judgment and bind your love for your child in chains, the guilt-imps *must* be conquered and banished into oblivion. You must be able to say and to believe, "It is done. Yesterday's dreams were for yesterday; today I will start with what I have today. I will not look back; 'if only' belongs to the past."

4. Hostility

AFTER THE SHARP, painful anguish of grief has subsided, and the parents have begun to acknowledge the reality of their child's handicap and defeated the first gnawing guilt-imps, their attention turns to the cause of the deficiency and the person responsible. They begin to feel the stirrings of anger because this has happened, and if this anger is not controlled, the parents will find their progress along the road to acceptance blocked by another emotional reaction — hostility.

When allowed to grow, hostility can create a wall around the heart and prevent constructive thoughts. Because unchecked hostility can lead to bitterness and unhappiness for all concerned, it can be more destructive than any of the other negative emotions.

What is hostility? We all have a vague understanding of the emotion, and dictionaries define the word as: "pertaining to an enemy; a deep-seated hatred or the expression of ill will; directing a feeling of ill will or bad feeling in the form of threats or violent action against the object of the hostility." Hostility is that deep, long-lasting, cold hatred that grows from anger.

While grief and guilt are personal and inward-directed emotions, hostility is directed outward toward someone else. In order to feel hostile toward someone, a reason must be found to blame that person for the wrong he is believed to have committed. (Blame, according to the dictionary definition, means: "to hold responsible, to accuse, to place responsibility for something on a person; to hold someone responsible for something bad or wrong.)

Blaming the Doctors

The first person to be blamed by the parents is usually the doctor. When the handicap is the result of a birth defect or injury, there seem to be built-in and obvious reasons for blaming the doctor who delivered the baby. Statements such as these go on and on through the parents' minds — "If only the doctor had taken better care of my wife (or of me) before the baby was born, he'd have known something was going wrong and could have prevented it," "If only the doctor had not taken so long to get to the hospital, he'd have been there early enough to keep something from happening," "If he'd had enough sense not to use so much anesthesia," or, "He should have kept my baby in the incubator longer." Parents also go through the same pattern of blaming the physician when the handicap is a result of illness or accident — "If my child had been given better medical care, this would not have happened" and so on.

When anger toward the doctor is allowed to grow, hostility gives rise to distrust, and the enemy eventually becomes the entire medical profession. When this happens both the child and the parents suffer, for then medical attention may be rejected regardless of the need. The parents refuse to immunize their child; medical diagnosis as to the true cause and the treatment of the handicap is rejected; treatment in times of serious illness may even be refused. These are only a few examples of the actions of some parents, but they illustrate how the pattern of blame can increase the danger of more injury to the child.

The best way to halt this rise of hostility against doctors seems to be through knowledge of the handicap itself, because knowledge increases understanding, and understanding lessens blame. So talk to your doctor; let him know that you are more concerned about understanding the handicap itself than you are in finding a reason for holding him responsible for the cause.

(Remember, doctors are human, too, and he may have his own guilt-imps that are plaguing him with his share of the responsibility for what has happened.)

Now it is certainly true that sometimes the parents' blame and distrust of one particular doctor is justifiable, for mistakes in judgment do occur. But even in those rare instances when the cause of the deficiency can be traced directly to incompetent medical care, what will a feeling of hostility accomplish for either the parents or their child? Would it not be more beneficial for that energy to be expended on the effort to help the child?

Of course, you should not stay with a doctor whom you do not trust, but do be aware of the dangers of "doctor shopping." You will waste valuable time and much needed money by trying to find a doctor who will say what you want to hear. The time for searching for the cure is past; now your intent should be to find a doctor who is equipped through training and personality to care for your child.

Parents also feel hostile toward a doctor because of what he said to them. Human nature being what it is, no one feels warm toward the person who is the bearer of bad news. There is a part of every parent of a handicapped child, I suppose, that will forever feel a bit hostile toward the doctor who first told us that our child is deficient. Disappointment and fear form a stiff resistance to accepting the truth of this diagnosis, but today there are so many ways of testing even a very young child that only in rare cases is a faulty diagnosis made. So when a doctor tells you that your child lacks normal ability, you can be sure that he is telling you the truth. Sometimes it is hard to know the extent of the deficiency in the beginning, but you and the child will gain so much more if you work under the premise that he *is* deficient.

Actually, more to blame is the tenderhearted doctor who recognizes evidence of the deficiency and "kindly" does not tell the parents, or else assures them that they are "only being too concerned" when they express their fears to him. When your feelings persist (and usually they will, for deep inside parents sense when something is wrong with their child), talk to the doctor, ask about special tests, or ask his opinion about consulting a specialist. Time can be very important in the treatment, therapy, and training with many types of handicaps — even mental retardation.

Hostility toward Teachers and Therapists

Sometimes parental hostility is directed toward those who are working with the child — the teachers and therapists. The parents know that their child is "slow," but believe that he should be showing more progress in his development. Someone must be at fault, the parents think, so it must be those who are responsible for his training. When you find yourself blaming the teachers or therapists because your child's progress is slower than you believe it should be, perhaps that is the time to seek a reevaluation of his ability. Don't sit around and complain — do something constructive. Realize that behind your anger lie disappointment and the frustration of not knowing what you should do, or what you should expect. You may be expecting too much from your child's limited capability; or, perhaps he really does need to change to a different type of program. But, if you let anger and blind blame grow into cold hostility, nothing good will be accomplished, for hostility is a one-way street that leads only to a blank wall of bitter frustration and unhappiness.

It is when a teacher is the first to tell parents that their child is deficient in ability, that hostility most often develops toward educators. Frequently, a child's lack of ability does not become apparent until he is in school. This is particularly true with children who have perceptual problems, minimal brain damage, or when the child is a slow learner. So it is the teacher who is the first to notice the deficiency. (Or is this really so? Haven't his parents been just a little concerned about the child's development all along?) Now, I'm not advocating that you accept the diagnosis of the first teacher who tells you that your child should be placed in the special education class. What I am saying is that the parents should not let her words go unheeded. Take steps to find out if what she says is valid, for not until you know for sure through testing and evaluation by someone trained and qualified to do so, can a wise decision be made. Don't fight the teacher, though, and don't put the blame on her or the school for not teaching or understanding your child. Rather, be thankful that she cared enough to give you her opinion.

Hostility toward the Other Parent

In the search to find the cause of the deficiency and to shift the eye of blame away from self, the next object of blame may well be the other parent. The question, "Is there some weakness in your ancestry which could have caused this?" leads to the question, "What weakness did my child inherit from you that caused this to happen?" Even when heredity may be a factor, such as in Down's syndrome, and a genetic incompatability results in mental retardation; or when the Rh negative factor is present in the blood of one parent and contributed to mental retardation — what good will blame accomplish? Absolutely none!

When the handicapping deficiency follows an illness or accident, there is, of course, a more direct reason for placing blame on the parent who was involved. Since this parent is usually the mother, the father may hurl accusations at her, often at the same time that she is trying to overcome her feelings of guilt. Here, as in the cases of birth defects, blame accomplishes nothing good or constructive. The damage cannot be undone, regardless of the effort. Far better to turn your love for each other and for your child into a cooperative effort that will help him. Far better to reassure each other and to help resolve any feelings of guilt, for when blame toward the other parent is allowed to grow, true hostility develops. Then the walls of resentment are built tall and strong and strengthened day by day until, where once there was love and respect between the parents, coldness and rejection take over and the family unit eventually breaks apart.

Living under the shadow of hostility, the mother finds insidious ways to "punish" the father; ways that are at first unconscious, then deliberate. She may begin to be less of a wife by withholding affection and, finally, sex. In her hostility she grows increasingly more negative, complaining, and nagging to find an outlet for her bitterness. Love cannot exist in such a climate, so family harmony is destroyed and a once good relationship deteriorates into war — or, at best, an open truce.

Fathers, too, punish their wives for "causing this to happen," and their ways can be just as devious and sometimes even more destructive to the family. Most frequently, these punishing actions are unconscious rather than deliberate, but when prompted by hostility the results are just as destructive. For example, he comes home from work too tired to do anything except collapse in his chair in front of the television or fall asleep on the couch after dinner — a dinner that he may have complained about; or, he doesn't come home until late at night because "there is so much to do at the office"; or, his weekly game with the boys becomes nightly. He may turn down his wife's pleas to go out together with perfectly reasonable sounding excuses which are completely invalid — his hidden desire being to punish her. Unchecked hostile feelings do not go away, they only grow worse. While husbands have been known to give action to their hostility through physical violence toward their wives, the more frequently encountered retaliation is leaving home. Sick with remorse, depressed by his failure, his battered psyche can take no more assaults to his ego; blame has caused many divorces.

I don't mention these examples to frighten you, just to make you aware of what can happen when unresolved blame grows into cold hostility. Do you see any glimmer of yourself or your actions in what has been said? All right, stop right now and take stock. Listen to your conscience — is it trying to tell you something? For your child's sake, you must work to resolve these feelings and to put a halt to the destructive actions. Every child needs two parents who love and respect each other and who work together to create a happy and secure home atmosphere. Because he is so dependent upon his family, the handicapped child needs this security even more than a nonhandicapped child may because he has less ability to withstand tension. Handicapped children often possess an uncanny sensitivity to the emotions of those people who are close to them. Regardless of the type of deficiency, your child has his own job to do in fighting the battle — don't make it any harder for him!

When a child is handicapped, there are enough causes for tension and unhappiness for the parents. For goodness sake, don't make your task any harder by fighting each other. Life with a handicapped child *can* be happy, and productive, and worthwhile. You do have to exert more effort than some other couples seem to require, but any goal which you have to work to attain becomes more worthwhile and more precious. So don't think for a minute that without a handicapped child, you would not have to work to make your marriage a success.

There are instances, of course, when the adjustment simply cannot be made, when feelings of hostility cannot be held in check. If this should happen in your family, remember that there are well-trained and experienced professional people to counsel you. Seek their help.

Parental Hostility and the Child

Another person toward whom the parents' hostility may be directed is, of course, the child himself. All parents have hostile feelings toward their children at times and "take out" these feelings on their children. Parents of nonhandicapped children are driven to frustration and spank a child too hard, or yell, or in anger inflict punishment which is too severe. This type of parental action isn't right, or even desirable, but that is part of being a parent — all parents are human, and all make mistakes. But when this kind of action becomes more than a once-in-a-while occurrence or is really physically harmful to the child, then it is unhealthy and can actually be dangerous. Because of their child's handicap, the parents are placed under unusual stress and strain; the frustrations are more constantly present. Just as this is true, so also must the parents of handicapped children place unusual restraint upon their reactions. Understanding the causes of your feelings helps you to learn to recognize and control your hostile reactions. Your child's handicap does not grant you above average capability to handle tension and frustration, rather, this life-role of yours demands that you learn to control your reactions.

Resentment is one of the causes of hostile feelings toward your child, and one of the causes of your resentment is that he is a hindrance to your social life. Now, this may seem to be a minor consideration, but as time passes it grows more significant. Man is a social creature and needs contact with other people. With many types of handicaps, as the child grows older it becomes increasingly more difficult for the parents to participate in their usual social activities. Reliable baby sitters are hard to find, budgets sometimes just cannot be made to stretch to pay for child care, and the child is too old to take out, or else it just isn't possible. Perhaps even good friends begin to show that they are uncomfortable in the presence of the child. The parents, especially the mother, begin to feel that the walls of the house are closing in on them. Hostility toward the child develops and grows until both parents resent his very existence.

Other parents who have handicapped children have found ways to relieve these restrictions. Some have changed the type of recreation — perhaps a picnic in a park rather than a night out on the town; walking or bicycling with the child along, rather than bowling or tennis or golf. Instead of dining out, the money can be used to prepare a special meal and invite a few friends in after the child is in bed. (Fathers, did you realize that one of the reasons mothers enjoy eating out is that they don't have to clean the kitchen afterward? So, by washing the dishes, you will make the occasion a real party for her, and she'll love and appreciate you all the more. Or, what about going one step further and learning to cook? Gourmet cooking is a hobby many men enjoy.)

You may be saying, "But we can't even attend church together because of our child." If this is important to you, look for a church that provides a nursery and will take an overage child, or perhaps a Sunday school class for handicapped children. If your church has no such facilities, you might work toward organizing one. One of the best ways to overcome resentment and hostility is to put that energy to work in a positive action. One mother I know, whose son is severely handicapped because of cerebral palsy, organized a nursery class especially for handicapped children in her church's Sunday school program. This class later grew into a Sunday school class attended by handicapped children of other denominations. Soon after that class was well established, she and her husband, with the help of other parents who had handicapped children and other interested friends, established a day camp at a friend's nearby farm. That camp grew into a week-long residential camp for handicapped youngsters with professionally trained counselors to supervise the teenage counselors. Now, spearheaded by a group from her local church, the national organization of her denomination is building a greatly needed residential school for handicapped children in this area of the state.

Unusual? Of course, it is. But after all, we parents who have handicapped children *are* unusual, aren't we? And if we weren't to begin with, we have certainly learned to be!

But you are right; that particular case is unusual, and the parents are truly exceptional people. I used this example just to show you what can be accomplished when positive thinking leads to constructive action. The point is, don't just sit there in your house and mope about the hard deal that life has handed out to you. Get up and do something constructive! Believe me, nothing turns off the destructive effects of hostility as effectively as constructive action.

It is at home that resentment toward the handicapped child is most likely to flare into open hostility. Regardless of the type or the severity of the deficiency, when a child is handicapped, extraordinary demands are placed on both parents. For the mother, there are the tasks of caring for the child's needs which may physically exhaust her. Tired, emotionally drained by the frustration of not really knowing what to do to help her child and his development, despondent because she can see no end to this way of life, the mother has little left of herself for her husband, herself, or the rest of the family.

Disappointment plays a large part in the mother's feelings, too. She notices an adorable, blondhaired little girl in the grocery store and thinks to herself, "Why couldn't my daughter be like that?" She watches the daughters of her friends grow and knows that she will never have the opportunity to see her daughter thrill the stands with her cheerleader's pep and vitality or help her dress for her first prom — and on and on her train of thought goes until she feels the bitter gall of disappointment turn into resentment against her child. No need for her head to tell her that her feelings are only natural, guilt-imps still plague her thoughts. Afraid of what others (including her husband) may think of her for feeling as she does, she hides her feelings: hidden, they grow out of proportion and become manifested in hostility toward her child.

The father, disappointed, too, because of his shattered dreams for his child also feels the pangs of guilt. He looks at his infant son and knows he never will see him make the winning touchdown, or send the baseball soaring over the field; he'll never see his son handed his college diploma, and there will be no future extension of himself and his accomplishments. And his disappointment leads to guilt, and his guilt makes him resent his child because he is ashamed of his feelings. Not only must the father deal with his disappointment, he also has the worry of additional financial burdens to meet. He sees the future stretching out in an endless effort to provide money for the extra care and treatment for his child, and worry becomes fear. The fear leads to resentment and blame and from there to hostility toward the child — and he feels guilty about his feelings.

Guilt because of resentment leads to ambivalence — the love-hate conflict that is the most destructive reaction of all. Ambivalence is sneaky, because it can make you believe that you are doing what is best for your child, when in truth you are hindering your child's progress and threatening his happiness. The pattern of ambivalence runs something like this: feeling guilty about their resentment of their child, the parents compensate by overprotecting him. Because the child expresses a dislike of the medicine, it is stopped; because the exercises make him fret, they are stopped; the braces are uncomfortable, so they are discarded. The child cries or throws a temper tantrum whenever he is thwarted, so the parents give in to his every whim and good discipline goes out the window. By using these "kind" tactics to cover up their resentment, the parents are instrumental in hindering their child's progress because advancement is impossible and what potential the child has lies undeveloped. Or, to protect the child from those who might not treat him "right," he is shielded from social contacts, which can also mean that he is shielded from those who might help him — the therapists and teachers.

On the other hand, parents may overreact, not realizing that they are actually punishing their child because of his deficiency. Exercises are too strenuously done and cries of pain are ignored; a bad-tasting medicine is administered rather than one that would be better tasting and just as effective. Or, discipline may be too strict, and punishment too severe; demands for behavior and performance may be unrealistically high for the child's ability. The child then reacts with human defiance, frustration becomes overpowering, and tempers are lost. In anger the parents may strike the child too hard and actually harm him.

Now that some of the results of unchecked ambivalence have been considered, what can be done to prevent the effects? First, consider this: the object of your hostility is not the child, it is the handicapping deficiency. Knowing this, learn all that you can about your child's type of handicap, for with knowledge will come understanding that will increase your own self-confidence and reassurance in your ability to handle the situation. Talk to the doctors, let them know that you are trying to gain a clearer understanding of the full scope of your child's handicap. The teachers and therapists at a clinic that specializes in your child's type of deficiency are another good source of information. Books contain a wealth of information, but frequently can be too technical, so learn to sift out that information you need at the time. Talking with other parents is frequently most helpful, for many times you will learn practical information which will help you gain an insight into the solution of your problem. Also, you will realize that your feelings of disappointment and resentment are only normal, and that you therefore have less reason to feel guilty.

While there is seldom any way to know exactly what can be expected from your child's progress, methods of testing have been developed that do give a pretty reliable indication of the limits he is capable of reaching, as well as the potentialities according to the degree of damage your child has suffered. For example, if nerve and muscle involvement is such that your child cannot sit alone, it is generally useless to expect that he will be capable of being toilet-trained, and you will only add to your own and your child's frustration by expecting him to accomplish this. Or, if the muscles and nerves in his neck and throat have been damaged so that his speech has not developed in the normally expected pattern, the child's drooling might simply be due to his lacking the ability to control his swallowing muscles.

As you learn to work within the limits of your child's ability, you will find that your frustration will lessen. As you learn to forget about blame, you will then be more able to find the right balance between love and protection; and released from the restriction of hostility and frustration, you will be freed to express your natural love toward your child. Most important of all, perhaps, you will find that when you have broken down the wall hostility has built around your heart, you can then hear the thoughts that will guide you in the right direction. Relieved of the burden of hostility, you will then be able to build the warm, loving family that will provide happiness and security for all.

5. Withdrawal

ONE OF THE DEFINITIONS given for the word withdraw in *The American Heritage Dictionary* is: "to remove oneself from activity or a social or emotional environment." Applying this definition to parents of handicapped children, withdrawal is cutting oneself off from social contact with other people.

A time of withdrawal is necessary for all of us at times. In solitude we can sort our thoughts and come to grips with our emotions so that we are able to develop the necessary inner strength to handle our reactions effectively. This is then a period of recuperation, vitally necessary for the body as well as for the mind. The desire to be alone is natural after an emotional crisis of any kind. But when this time extends past the quieting-down and solution-finding stage, and the same thoughts of fear and despair run on a never-ceasing mental treadmill, then withdrawal becomes neither useful nor helpful. Being alone becomes too easy, and daydreams too comforting an escape from reality. It is easier to stay away from people in the peace and safety of the home, isolated from the questions and the reactions of the outside world.

Withdrawal is a defense mechanism (a form of behavior that is adopted for the purpose of finding relief from the distress caused by some type of conflict) by which the parents build up their emotional stamina against the onslaught of despair and fear which full recognition of the reality of their child's handicap might bring. Like grief and guilt, withdrawal is a personal emotion, for it concerns self; like denial and hostility, the individual's state of mind can greatly affect those around him.

It is when withdrawal is used as an escape mechanism that it becomes dangerous and unhealthy. By disassociating oneself from people and the unprotected real world outside the home, it is easy to fall into the trap of fantasy, pretending that the handicap does not exist. But it is not necessary to stay at home to escape reality by withdrawal. One can continue to function alongside other people and withdraw into the mind so that the walls keep out reality just as effectively as the actual brick walls of the home. So, in withdrawal, one can physically remove himself from his social environment (people), or he can mentally remove himself from his emotional environment. Either way, it is still a barrier blocking progress toward acceptance and adjustment.

Falling into the Trap of Withdrawal

Withdrawal is usually more of a problem for the mother; the father must go out into the world and be among people in order to earn a living, while the mother's child-care responsibilities provide reason for her to stay at home. (Although fathers, too, have ways of withdrawing which will be discussed later.)

Withdrawal usually creeps up on the mother of a handicapped child, and she doesn't realize that her self-sought isolation is a great contributing factor to the feeling of depression she is experiencing. At first, caring for her child in his illness, or caring for the newborn infant, fills her day and is a natural deterrent for the desire to socialize. But as time goes on, she begins to hesitate to leave her child alone lest something happen, and she feels that she can trust no one else to provide the proper care. (Also, perhaps, because she has rebuffed her friends' offers of help and friendship, they have taken her at her word and are leaving her alone.) Going out with the child means too many questions to answer, too much explaining to do, and so it is easier to stay at home within the safety of the quiet and unquestioning walls. Or, the mother may be afraid she'll lose control over her emotions and cry too easily and too frequently in the wrong places in front of the wrong people. After all, even with this tragedy, she can't wear her heart on her sleeve and become Weeping Winifred at the expense of everyone else's embarrassment.

So, the aloneness of solitude becomes a habit, and the stage of withdrawal sets in. Now there is nothing wrong with being antisocial, with preferring solitude to the company of other people — except, that it really isn't very healthy. Man is a social animal and being so needs the exchange of ideas, interest beyond his own doorstep, and the concern for other people that only socializing will bring to him. Without such interchange, one becomes self-centered and indrawn, and this can be extremely damaging to the whole family. Why? Well, for one reason, when you have nothing to think about but your own problems, those problems become magnified in your own mind until they grow all out of proportion.

"But I need more time. I'm not ready to face the outside world yet," you say? But you have to *make* yourself ready. You have no more time to waste. Listen carefully to what your conscience is saying — now, are you really content and happy?

Take a good look at your child who is handicapped. What are you doing for him? What are you in your self-imposed exile from the human race doing *to* him? Have you begun a constructive program of therapy for him? Are you being sure that he is receiving the quality of medical care he needs? Or, are you sitting there at home, just looking at him, taking care of his physical needs and crying because there is "something wrong" with him?

Are there other children in the family? If so, are you being a good mother to them? Or, are you letting your mood of depression and despair carry over to them so that they, too, feel the weight of the burden of your handicapped child? Does your lack of interest in anything outside the house or anyone other than your handicapped child include also the accomplishments and needs of your nonhandicapped children? Your other children, whether younger or older, can understand and accept, for a time, why their handicapped brother or sister needs your time and concern more than they do, but before long they will begin to feel left out, and their sense of security is threatened because they are no longer assured of their mother's love for them.

And there is your husband. Are you being fair to him? Are you giving him the love and interested concern he needs? He, too, has been hurt; he, too, would like to hide but cannot for he must go out into the world to make a living. Are you so wrapped up inside your cloak of withdrawal that you've left him outside your awareness? He needs you and depends upon you to help him. Above all, he needs your love, and the chilly atmosphere of withdrawal can provide a very successful damper to even the warmest love. Your withdrawal from people in the outside world can lead to your withdrawal from your husband. You need his love and concern, and the more you withdraw from him, the harder it is for him to show you that he loves you and is concerned about your needs. Love withers in such an atmosphere just as much as in hostility, because withdrawal leads to hostile thoughts.

Of course, it is hard for you to shake loose these feelings you have! It's difficult for you to muster up the courage to re-enter the world! Who ever said that it is easy? But you must — for your own good, as well as for the sake of your handicapped child and for your entire family. Your own happiness and your well-balanced emotional outlook are very important, because, like it or not, the emotional climate in your home depends upon you, for every member of your family reflects and is affected by your moods and attitude.

How do you know when you are in this withdrawal stage? These are some of the symptoms: not making an effort to see friends, not leaving the home or having company in, excusing antisocial behavior because of a variety of reasons which are not really valid (being too busy, the furniture needs recovering, can't afford to entertain, et cetera). Do you believe that you're content passing the idle hours by watching just anything on the television (even children's cartoon shows), and yet hardly remembering what it was that you saw? Or, if you read, do you read only light, "escape" material and forget it as soon as you turn the pages or close the book? Do you find yourself staring out the window or at an empty wall for long periods of time, daydreaming — perhaps of what life will be when your child is "all right" again? Another symptom is losing awareness of oneself — little or no make-up, not even when your husband comes home from work; hair arranged just any sort of way; clothes ill-fitting or not clean and neat. Also, housekeeping is left to go to pot, so to speak — the beds are unmade (who will see them, anyway?), the breakfast dishes are left unwashed, the clutter of normal living allowed to pile up and the dust to lie undisturbed. If this line of action (or nonaction) is followed, the intellect loses the ability to function at the usual level, for when not used, the mind can fall into a state of atrophy where the ability to concentrate, to make decisions, to think constructively deteriorates. But rest assured, the mind *can* recover, if you will begin to use it.

"But I'm always so tired; I just don't have the energy to do my housework; I'm too tired even to care what I look like," are frequently heard excuses. Mothers caught in this trap then begin to nap more often, and the naps last longer and longer, and still they are tired. Why? Perhaps because they have nothing interesting, pleasant, or different to look forward to, and so they are bored — and boredom breeds fatigue.

If any of these symptoms fits you and your state of mind, stop! Do something toward taking constructive steps to change before the walls of your safe, secure home become prison walls. Solitude is often a habit, a rut that is easy to fall into but hard to climb out of. The longer one stays away from people, the harder it becomes to gather the courage needed to shut the front door *behind* one and walk out into the world of people.

The story of Mary and Bart K. and their two children is an example of what can happen when parents, especially mothers, let withdrawal remain a stumbling block to their adjustment to having a child who is handicapped. In the early years of their marriage, the K.'s were a popular couple with a wide circle of friends. Bart's quiet, confidence-inspiring manner provided the perfect complement to Mary's bubbling vivaciousness. He was a promising young attorney, a "man with a future"; she was a high school teacher whose art classes were always filled to overflowing. Both were outgoing and friendly, interested in and involved with community affairs and active members of their church, where they worked with the young people. After their first child, George, was born, Mary and Bart continued their involvement in church and community affairs. Life was happy and fulfilling; Bart's career was advancing rapidly, Mary reveled in her role of wife and mother and homemaker; George was a happy, well-adjusted "bundle of sunshine."

But when George was nearly three years old, Susie was born, and suddenly their happy and secure life became dark and gloomy. Susie was mongoloid; she had Down's syndrome, caused by a genetic incompatability of the parents, although the cause was not known at that time. Their friends rallied around and tried to help, but Mary turned down all overtures of sympathy or concern. She and Bart turned down invitations and dropped out of their clubs and organizations. They entertained no more. Their minister tried to help, but the K.'s stopped attending church. When their doctor made an appointment for Mary with the Family Counseling Service, she canceled the appointment and changed physicians. Finally, when Susie was about one year old, they moved across country to a large city, and their old friends lost contact with them.

All this I know only through hearsay, because when I first met the K.'s Mary was a bitter, unhappy person; her closed-in, angry expression belied her once happy and outgoing nature, and her ill-fitting, frumpy dress with split seams and dangling hem accentuated her overweight. Bart was a stooped, silent man and his face had that hangdog look so often worn by people who have been defeated by their problems. The K.'s had made very few friends since moving to this city, and most of these were "only acquaintances," Mary said. Although Susie was nine, she was not in school for Mary did not like the special classes in the public schools because "they don't really teach the kids anything, and the other children at school make fun of those in special ed." Although she had attempted to teach Susie at home, the child was poorly coordinated physically, had almost no speech, and her constant sullen attitude was indicative of a very unhappy little girl. George was a withdrawn, shy child who, although he could not seem to get along with other children, was doing quite well in seventh grade. The family neither attended church nor belonged to any civic or social organizations. Bart was no longer practicing law, but was working at a job that he obviously did not like and offered no challenge to his capabilities. Mary no longer painted or used her artistic talent in any way.

I wish I could report a happy ending to this story, but I cannot and still be truthful. Susie is now sixteen and the happiest member of the family. Three years ago, Mary and Bart realized that she would be much happier in a residential school situation, and here she has had a chance to lead a life that is normal for her. Her speech has greatly improved, she is learning to read, and can now follow simple directions. George is working, and although his job is far below his level of ability, at least he is staying out of trouble. His high school education was interrupted when he was arrested for petty theft and possession of narcotics. Thanks to court-ordered psychotherapy, he seems to be straightening out his thinking and coming to grips with his life. Mary has resumed her painting, and perhaps if she can overcome her mental anguish and hostility, which is too much reflected in her work, she will then be free to express her truly exceptional talent. Bart has resigned himself to trudging along in his job until he reaches retirement age. They still live a life of isolation and have very few, if any, friends.

The ending could have been worse, certainly, for the K.'s seem to be finally finding some happiness, and, of course, the end of their story has not yet been determined. But think of what their lives could have been, for they started out with so much promise. Mary's withdrawal from society was not the only determining factor, for there were other negative attitudes and reactions, but it certainly contributed to a home atmosphere that fostered and nurtured negative reactions and attitudes.

Now, compare the K.'s story with that of the L.'s. There was nothing particularly outstanding about Kathy and Ned, not in the way of shining talent or above average ability, but they carried about them an aura of cheerfulness and friendliness and even a sort of suppressed but confident hopefulness. Their son Billy was four years old when their long awaited daughter, Kimberly, was born. She was perfect — a beautiful, chubby little charmer. When she was three weeks old, her sniffles turned out to be not the mild cold her parents thought, but encephalitis. For weeks the doctors fought to save her life. They were successful, but the high fever and raging infection damaged Kimberly's brain, and even before she was a year old, the doctors were able to diagnose cerebral palsy and possible severe mental retardation. Their family and friends also rallied around Kathy and Ned, but they listened to the advice they were given, and welcomed all the overtures of friendship and sympathy. Billy was encouraged to visit his grandparents as well as other boys his age whom he met at the nursery school he attended, and he was encouraged to bring his friends home to play. Rather than turn away from their church, the L.'s became even more involved, and little Kimberly accompanied her mother to meetings, winning the hearts of all who met her and becoming "Queen of the Nursery." When Kimberly was old enough to begin therapy, Kathy took her to the clinic for treatments. Anytime she could not be home when Billy came in from school, there were a dozen or so friends she could call upon to take him to their homes for lunch and play. The L.'s attended meetings of the parents' group at the clinic, and when they learned about other families in their part of the city who had similar problems, Kathy started a car pool to the clinic and enlisted volunteers to drive those children whose parents could not manage transportation. Kathy and Ned organized a group of their friends and other parents of handicapped children as a sort of clearing-house of information and sources of help for parents who were newcomers and who had handicapped children. (This service was eventually taken over by Kathy's guild at her church.) When Kimberly was four years old, the tests showed her mental ability to be only at the trainable level and her physical impairment to be moderate. The L.'s then made the difficult decision to place her in the nearby branch of the State School for Retarded Children, where she could receive the extensive training and therapy she required, and where she could have friends and a life pattern she could handle. Also, Billy was growing older, and although he loved his sister and showed little or no resentment toward her, he needed more of his parents' time than they were able to give him and still meet Kimberly's needs.

Kimberly has been in school two years now; her visits home, brief and infrequent on the advice of the school staff, are happy and fun-filled for the entire family. Billy is a Cub Scout in Kathy's den and plays ball on the team that Ned coaches. They still have adjustment problems at times, but the periods of depression are becoming shorter, less intense, and farther apart. Both parents continue to be active members of the area organization for parents of handicapped children and are "on call" to help other parents when needed. They are expecting another child in a few months, and although Billy wants a brother, I'm sure a sister will be just as welcome.

No, it was not easy for Kathy and Ned to accept their

daughter's handicap. In many aspects it was a particularly hard task for them, because they had to fight their guilt of feeling responsible for Kimberly's illness. But with the support of their friends and the guidance and counseling of their minister and doctors, Kathy and Ned were able to strengthen their own inner resources and develop their ability to cope with their problems. If either had withdrawn, guilt and resentment, hostility and blame no doubt would have grown and ruined the family. Not one of these four lives was wasted, and they have given much to so many people. Their future is bright and filled with purpose and hope.

Climbing Out of the Rut of Withdrawal

It is easy to fall into the rut of withdrawal, but how can one climb out? The first step is to understand that falling into the rut is passive, nonaction; climbing out of the rut is active, the effort must be exerted to pull oneself up. You can and will receive help from others — your husband (or wife), your family and friends, the doctors, your minister or rabbi — but you must take the first step yourself and realize that this is necessary for the survival of your entire family. In other words, you must want, or make yourself want, to leave the sanctuary of your house and welcome the intrusion of other people into your private world.

Let us start first with mothers. The secret to success is to begin small. Telephone a close friend, inviting her to come over for coffee or tea. Explain why you've acted as you have — something like this perhaps: "Because of the trouble we've had with the baby (or with Mark or Carolyn, if your child is older), I just haven't felt like being with people. Things are better now, and I want to see you." By taking this approach, you've told your friend several important things that will help her feel more relaxed. You've let her know that she hasn't been responsible for your attitude; you've told her that you know "something is wrong" with your child, and she doesn't have to worry about how she is going to avoid the issue in her conversation; and you've let her know that you're ready to come back into the world and have chosen her as your first contact. You've taken the affirmative approach and, by so doing, have done much to relieve her uneasiness.

Now, you can straighten up the house, or at least the kitchen and the living room. You have a reason now to arrange your hair, to put on make-up, to change into attractive clothes — you have company coming! (By the way, if your friend should have other plans that prevent her from accepting your first invitation, don't be super-sensitive and let this squelch your attempt for a coming out — either give her another invitation or phone someone else.) When your guest arrives, you might steer the conversation away from your child, if that bothers you too much right now, by asking her to tell you about what she has been doing and to bring you up-to-date on the activities of your other friends.

There are other constructive steps you can take for yourself. Become involved in doing something interesting — a handcraft project, perhaps, for your house or for Christmas gifts; learn to do one of the various kinds of needlework; try your hand at knitting or crocheting. You might begin planning to update your wardrobe — a new dress or even a new blouse or scarf to revive an old outfit can provide a tremendous lift to sagging spirits. Or, how about learning to sew? Since your budget may be strained almost to the breaking point, this is one of the easiest and most gratifying ways to cut expenses. Or think about redecorating your house. What about cooking — experiment with Chinese cooking or a new French dessert?

Do change your reading habits; really read the daily newspaper so you will have some idea of what is going on in your community and in the world. Go to the library and check out a book that will challenge your mind and get the rust out of your thinking. (You might peruse the paperback book rack at the grocery store. You'll find a wealth of informative books there for a nominal price.)

These suggestions are made to prepare you for going out and being with people again. (If you have a job outside the home, you are already with people, but you might find some of the suggestions useful during your at-home hours. Many mothers do not work outside their homes, and the following suggestions are more applicable to them.) If your budget can be stretched to pay a baby sitter, or if a relative or friend is willing to baby-sit, give yourself a treat of a few hours away from the house and your child once a week — even once a month is beneficial. Ask your husband to baby-sit occasionally so you can get out and be with friends or go shopping. You will have to learn to trust someone else with the care of your child eventually, you know, and believe me, you will be a much better mother when you come back home. If your child is attending a clinic, the parents' group there offers an excellent opportunity for you. They have all been through the same circumstances as you are now going through, and so they will not only understand how you feel, they will have many suggestions to offer which will be useful and helpful. If your child is still an infant, you can take him out just as mothers of other babies do — in a carriage or stroller. (If you do not have such a convenience and feel you cannot spare the money to buy one, check the "thrift shops" often sponsored by churches, or look in the "for sale" section of the newspaper. You can always clean and sterilize a used carriage or stroller.) This may be the right time for you to join a women's group in your church, and many churches provide nurseries so young mothers can attend guild or circle meetings.

It matters little what you do, only that you do something in which you will find satisfaction and a sense of purpose. You will, however, find a greater sense of purpose if you are doing something for someone else, whether it is packing boxes for needy orphans or collecting in your neighborhood for a fund drive. By the way, serving on the telephone calling committee is a very useful service in any organization, and a contribution you can make if you cannot easily leave the house.

Now, about that "I'm always tired" feeling you have. You might have a very valid medical reason for your fatigue, and it might not be "just in your mind" at all. Pick up the telephone and make an appointment with your doctor for a checkup. While you are in his office, you will also have an opportunity to talk to him about your worries. As a matter of fact, you should, because knowing how you feel emotionally helps him form a better picture of your physical condition.

Husbands Can Help

A mother needs her husband's support and help if she is to be successful in breaking her pattern of withdrawal. No one else is as close to your wife and in a position to understand the problems she faces as you are. Pay attention to your wife, notice what she is doing, and be aware of how she may have changed. Talk to her gently and with love, letting her know you care as you try to learn how she feels and why. Many times the person who has withdrawn is completely unaware of what has happened, so now is the time for you to begin to take constructive steps to help your wife climb out of the rut of her withdrawal.

What are some of the "constructive steps?" The secret of your success is to begin small. Be insistent about taking your wife out of the house, but not to a function that will put too many demands upon her. Choose something simple, such as a movie or dinner in a nearby restaurant. You make all the arrangements yourself — the baby sitter, the reservations, the day and time — and don't give your wife any opportunity to make excuses for not going. Once the arrangements are all made, she'll find it hard to justify canceling them. If she grumbles and tries to find excuses why she cannot or should not go, be patient with her. Make her understand that this is something that is important to you because you love her.

Another approach you might use is to give her a shopping

day. You know, deep down inside most women really like to shop, whether to buy something special or just to look. You are responsible enough to look after your handicapped child, so shoo your wife out of the house and you stay home. (Now, remember — this "day off" is your gift to your wife, so *you* clear away the breakfast dishes and make the beds and sweep the floor that day.) If she continues to balk at the idea of leaving her home and child for even a few hours, you might think of some needed purchase that only she can decide upon — something for the house, perhaps. Or, you might enlist the help of one of her friends, for women usually find that shopping with a companion along is more fun. It really doesn't matter what ruse you use to encourage your wife to get out of the house; shopping is merely one suggestion that often works because it is such a practical activity. You can accomplish the same purpose by making it possible for her to play bridge, go visiting, or see a movie — you only want to encourage her to take those first steps toward resuming her before-this-happened activities and interests.

Surely one of the most effective steps you can take to help your wife is to seek professional counseling for her. That old saying "An ounce of prevention is worth a pound of cure" was never more applicable than in this instance. If you are aware of your wife's withdrawal and depression at the beginning of this stage of reaction, then one session, or only a few, will probably be sufficient, but even if her withdrawal is well entrenched, a counselor will be able to help her. If you do not know how to go about finding a counselor trained in working with adults, begin by asking your (or her) doctor. Or, perhaps you can persuade her to talk to her doctor. In many localities a Family Counseling Service, or similar facility, is available for only a nominal cost. If you are churchgoers, talk to your minister. He is trained, sympathetic, already familiar with your family situation and is also aware of the services available in your community.

Don't forget gifts to your wife — presents from you that will help her want to go out. A new dress or scarf or sweater that you bought for her may be just the encouragement she needs.

Notice what is going on in your home, look at your wife with loving concern for her problems, and you will think of the right steps to take. Overlook the messy house, her unkempt appearance, the unappetizing meals she's been serving, and consider what might lie beneath her attitude. Then, follow your own instincts, for you can do more than anyone else to bring your wife out of her shell — or to keep her from retreating into that shell in the first place. Your wife may be efficient and an accomplished homemaker, she may appear not to need the stimulation of other people, but are you sure this is really how she feels inside, or if home is truly enough for her?

If your wife is not as interesting a companion as she once was, perhaps it is because she has not had access to new ideas and her mind has grown stale from lack of stimulation. Do you try to converse with her, or do you wait for her to begin the conversation? Do you use her only as a soundingboard for your own opinions and ideas? Instead of complaining that she has become cold and unloving and unresponsive, stop and think about how you have treated her. Are you doing enough to prove to her that you love her, that your feelings have not changed toward her, and that she is still the most important person in your life?

Her withdrawing from, even her lack of response to, your lovemaking overtures may be because she feels she is no longer important to you. Because you are more responsible for her attitude toward you than you realize, you must accept some of that responsibility. You will find a much lengthier discussion in the chapter "Especially for Husbands," but right here is a good place to remind you that a woman thrives on a man's love. For a wife, it is vitally necessary for her well-being that she feel secure in the knowledge her husband loves her and that she is important to him. She cannot function effectively as a woman, as a mother, and certainly not as a wife without this knowledge.

Escape from the Prison of Withdrawal

You cannot let yourself withdraw, whether from people in the world outside your home, or from your family inside your home. To do so is to turn your interest inward and to concentrate on yourself. Without the leveling counterbalance of other people's ideas, you will inevitably lose that all-important perspective that allows you to view your problems in the proper proportion. Losing this, you then lose the ability to take effective action toward solving those problems; you will reach that point of view when you can see nothing but the dark side of your life, and one unhappy day follows another until your moods of depression become a continual way of life. Having a child who is handicapped is enough reason for unhappiness; you surely do not need other reasons. Nor can you let yourself build this incident into a greater tragedy, and that is exactly what will happen, if you do not escape from the prison of withdrawal.

So make yourself find the courage to get out into the stream of living. It's a wide world out there, full of excitement and interesting people who have much to offer you and to whom you have much to give. Each time you come back into your home, you will bring with you something that will make your life richer and will help you make the lives of your family happier. Don't be afraid; take your progress one step at a time. Turn your thoughts away from yourself and from your worries, then you will be free to hear what your heart is saying.

6. Rejection

THE LAST OF THE stages of negative reactions which parents experience as they progress toward accepting the reality of their child's handicap is rejection. Often it is very difficult to distinguish between the emotional reactions that express hostility and those that reveal rejection because these two emotions are so similar. There is a difference, however, and this difference is worth noting because of the different underlying causes as well as the different outward manifestations of each. Hostility, remember, concerns feelings of ill will directed toward an enemy, manifested in the form of threats or violent actions against the person who is the object of the hostile feelings, and has to do with punishment or retaliation. Rejection, on the other hand, according to *The American Heritage Dictionary* definition is: "to refuse to consider, to refuse affection or recognition to a person; to discard as useless or defective."

Just as the other reactions occur and reoccur throughout the whole period of adjustment, so does rejection also weave in and out through the tapestry of reactions as parents struggle to accept the reality of their child's handicapping deficiency. Rejection is a feeling that encompasses and is caused by many circumstances and events. It can be a single event-caused action or a long term and increasingly consistent attitude. It is this attitude and the resulting actions directed toward the child which are important. Rejection breeds a host of other undesirable and negative emotional reactions, not the least of which is guilt.

This last stage of emotional reactions represents one final

effort on the parents' part in their fight against having to believe that their child's deficiency will prevent his leading a normal life. It is sort of catch-all stage in which the other emotional reactions thought to have been overcome rise again and cause new stumbling blocks. Up until now, there has been hope that this is not true — that a cure will be found, or that time will prove the diagnosis wrong, or that growth and treatment will mean development. No parent wants to believe his child is handicapped, that he will always be deaf or blind, that he will never walk and run as other children do, or that his inability to learn will forever deny him the right to grow to maturity. Regardless of what has happened before, the realization of the permanence of the handicapping deficiency of ability means heartbreak for parents.

Rejection, this "last ditch stand," is not prompted merely by the parents' unrealistic and selfish motives because their dreams have been shattered and their hopes and ambitions for their child thwarted, there is also the factor of their fear. Now, there is nothing superficial or unrealistic about this fear; the foundations are very real and deep, ranging from the parents' fear that they will not be strong enough physically or emotionally to cope with their child's problems and to do what is best for him, to being afraid of what the future will hold for their child and if he will be able to cope with his own problems. (And in their fear, parents often can see nothing but problems in the life ahead.) So before you berate yourself for your own feelings of rejection, understand that the real problem may well be pure and simple fear, and the underlying motive is your battle against succumbing to your fear. Your fear will not simply vanish; like guilt, fear must be admitted and then analyzed before it can be defeated. Also like guilt, fear can destroy the person. The best weapon against fear is understanding, and the only means by which you can gain understanding is through knowledge. So, let's examine and analyze the various aspects of rejection, using the definition of the word itself as a guide.

Rejection of the Reality of the Deficiency
(To Refuse to Consider)

In this instance it is not so much denying that the child actually lacks ability, rather it is not believing that the condition is permanent or not admitting the extent of the deficiency. Although they may have once faced and acknowledged the reality of their child's lack of ability (either mental or physical), there is no assurance that as time passes, the parents will not still have to guard against falling into the trap of disbelief. Time itself may dull their acute awareness of the fact that their child is less able than other children. Living with the situation day after day, the problem becomes familiar and the threatening aspects become less obvious as compensations are made. Actually, this is the way it must be, in some degree, or else we would become so overburdened that we would lose the ability to function. This type of attitude is, in essence, what "Acceptance" is all about.

Refusal to consider or acknowledge the extent of the child's handicapping lack of ability may cause parents to place a false value on his development and achievements, and his lagging behind in age-level achievements will be unrecognized. Handicapped children, like nonhandicapped children, do not follow a steady rate of progressive development. Development and learning come in spurts and remain on plateaus for indefinite periods of time. During those periods of rapid development, the parents may be deceived into believing that (1) their fears were unfounded and the tests were inaccurate; or (2) that the child has overcome his lack of ability or has grown out of it. I've often compared child development to climbing a mountain — the way upward is slow and tortuous over the rough terrain, and one even may slide backward at times; then the path follows a gentle slope and progress is swift; and when a plateau is reached, the resting time is often mistaken for a cessation of (developmental) progress. It is during the climb over the gentle slope that the parents may be deluded into believing that their child is not deficient, or that the handicapping condition has been overcome. For example, the child who is mentally retarded may learn, during this spurt of development, to count to ten, to recognize the basic colors, or to write his name, and the parents, encouraged by this sign of progress, begin to plan for the day when he will "catch up" and enter the regular classroom. Or, the child with dyslexia finally begins to read simple material, and the parents think, "He's cured. Now we can stop all these therapy and training sessions." The deaf child may, during such a progressive period, begin to show that he has learned the rudiments of lip reading, so his parents withdraw him from the special school and enter him into the regular public school, not realizing that he has much farther still to go. The same type of analogy may be also applied to children who have a physical disability.

But let me warn you — beware of these periods. Being human and loving your child you want so very desperately to believe that everything is all right, or at least that the picture is not so dark as you thought it to be. You want to prove to the doctors and to others that they were wrong in believing that your child could not overcome his handicap. But remember, all those tests that were administered to your child, all the consultations and observations by trained and experienced professional people, did prove beyond a reasonable doubt that your child *is* lacking in ability. You must give him the chance to learn and to develop those abilities he does have. You must continue the therapy, the treatments, the special training, because during that period of time when he is making such rapid progress in his development, his ability to learn is accelerated. Make the most of this opportunity, but don't push too hard. Let your child appreciate his successes, let him enjoy his feats of accomplishment now, for in the future he will need to draw on the strength your approval has given him.

Regardless of the type of handicap your child has, he will inevitably reach plateaus when he will seem to be making no progress at all. A slowing down in rate of development can be terribly depressing to parents; sliding backward can be demoralizing and frightening. *Every* child has these leveling-off times, but a handicapped child's slowdown is more noticeable because so much attention is paid to the rate of his progressive development. (People will ask the parent of a nonhandicapped child, "How does George like school?", while a handicapped child's parents are asked, "How is Susan doing in school?") With a child who is handicapped, every step forward represents a giant leap; every step backward seems to mean doom. If there is one thing parents who have handicapped children must learn, it is to have patience, and in few other instances is patience more necessary than when one's child seems to have reached the limit of his potentiality. What one sees and interprets as the end of progressive development is often not that at all, for development actually is going on in areas that are not visible or easily detected. Notice that when your child is growing taller, he doesn't seem to be learning as fast. Or when he is making more strides in learning, his physical growth has reached a slowing-down phase. When your child does reach a plateau, whether it is in mental growth or physical development, take him out from under the microscope; have patience that tomorrow or next week or next month, he will again resume progressive development. Relax, let go of your fears, and you will then be free to enjoy your child as he is.

Rejection or refusal to consider the reality of the handicap may be shown in still another manner — by parents refusing to believe their child is not capable of performing at the level they consider possible for him. In other words, expecting too much of their child's performance level and putting too much pressure on him by demanding that he reach that level. A child may be incapable of speaking clearly because of a physical speech impairment, yet his parents insist he is only lazy; or a child's inability to walk may be the result of muscle or nerve damage, not because he "just isn't trying hard enough." Children whose mental ability is impaired to a lesser degree suffer most from parental expectations that are too high, simply because it is often so very difficult to distinguish between lack of ability and lack of will. But don't think for a minute that unrealistic expectation and pushing a child is an attitude restricted to parents of handicapped children — keeping that delicate balance between encouragement and praise is one of the most difficult tasks for all parents.

There is no pat answer; the only tried and proven approach is to make the effort to learn enough about your child's limits of ability so you will be better equipped to assess his potential and to take the positive approach in your attitude toward him and his progress. It is the nature of children that they respond best to praise (isn't that also true of adults?), so never be stingy in the amount of praise you lavish upon your child. Encourage him, yes, but always liberally season your words of encouragement and urging with praise for what he has accomplished. Don't be afraid to let your heart rule your words.

There is, of course, the other extreme — when parents feel their child's ability is so limited that nothing could be gained by training or therapy. Perhaps, because they believe their child has so little mental ability, no effort is exerted in trying to teach him anything at all, and the parents continue to treat him almost as if he were a new-born baby. Or, because a child's physical impairment is so great, his parents make little or no effort to do the exercises that would strengthen his muscles. In other words, because the handicapped child is thought to be hopeless, his parents reject any plans for therapy and training for him.

"Hopeless" according to what standards? Those of the parents, of course. Sure, many, many handicapped children will never be able to develop to that level which is considered "normal" — if this were so, they would not be handicapped. But each child has the right to reach toward the level of accomplishment of which he is capable. Muscles atrophy (waste away) when not used. The nonhandicapped infant exercises his muscles naturally, but the physically disabled baby must be helped to flex and extend his. If everything is done for the older child so there is no need for him to use his arms or legs, then he will not, and the time will come when what ability was present will be lost. A mind that is not challenged or excited or interested, will not expand and grow regardless of the innate ability.

But what is the purpose, when a child has so very little ability and only a very limited potential for development? The purpose is to give him the chance to be happy and healthy. By not being helped to develop what ability he has, the child is being rejected. He is rejected as a person — with the right to grow and develop what ability he has to help him be happy and satisfied that he has worth as a human being.

"But his medical care costs so much we cannot afford therapy. What can we do?" Today, thank goodness, there are sources of help for parents caught in a financial bind because of the needs of their handicapped children. There are government agencies — state and federal — as well as privately endowed associations which fund clinics and therapy centers where the fees are based on ability to pay. Don't be proud — search out what is available in your area. Keep in mind that you are seeking help for your child. Use the information given in "Sources of Help" in the Appendix. These helping hands are not going to seek you out; you must ask for help yourself. When parents follow a line of nonaction, they are not rejecting the reality of the existence of their child's handicapping lack of ability, but they are rejecting the reality of the existence of ability, and this rejection can be just as cruel and detrimental as any other aspect of rejection.

Rejection of the Child (To Refuse Affection)

Rejection of the handicapped child by his parents is complex. It is dependent upon many variables in the parent's own background and personality, and even the type of handicap and the extent of the child's inability will determine the parents' reaction, as well as the manner by which they reveal their feelings of rejection.

Let me assure you that you are going to have feelings toward your child that may be termed "rejection." He may still be an infant and little different from all the other babies you see, so you react now with disdain as you declare, "Not me! I'll never not love my child — or show him that I love him." But there will come the time when you, too, will dislike your child; when you, too, will wish there were some way you could be absolved of the fact that he is yours. And there will be times when your rejection will march beneath other banners so that you cannot recognize the feeling for what it really is. Why am I so sure of this? Because I know only too well that when the extraordinary burdens — physical, emotional, financial — thrust upon you by your child's handicap become overwhelming, you will think to yourself, "If only I didn't have this child." Or on a particularly bad day you will think, "I don't believe I can take this any longer."

All parents reject their children at times — even parents of normal children. But as parents of handicapped children, our burdens are unusually heavy, and we have merited the right to feel rejection toward our children. Be reassured that you are no monster when you wish you did not have this child.

You are your child's parent; you cannot, with a clear conscience, deny that fact, but you can dream about being relieved of the burdens. The "urge to kill" is only a human rebellion against an adversity we cannot resolve; the "wish to abandon" the child is but another dream-wish of finding a way to be relieved of the problems. Sometimes, a parent finds he cannot cope with the added stress, and these urges and wishes are actually put into action; the child is abandoned either by one parent leaving the home (most often the father), or by being placed in an institution and forgotten. Hidden and pushed away from conscious thought, these urges are still dangerous because they can cause other negative emotional reactions which may lead to destructive action. Because these kinds of thoughts are so "bad" and detestable, you may fear that admission would destroy the image of yourself you try to present to others. Truthfully, you do not want to say what you are thinking, because you are ashamed of what you feel. But don't be so! Once you have admitted to someone how you feel, you will find that the wall around your heart and thoughts begins to melt away. You cannot be objective about your own self-doubts and detestable thinking, but someone else whom you trust may be able to show you that you are not so evil after all.

I well remember one time when our Kathy was about three and a half years old. Her personality was really beginning to take form, and in a most unlikable way. She was obstinate, irritable, and spiteful. She would also cry continuously for lengthy periods of time, two and three hours or more, day and night. No one could discover why she did this, and nothing that we tried to do for her seemed to help. She would fight and push me away when I tried to love her and responded only a little less violently to her father. Needless to say, her crying alone was enough to drive me crazy, and at times I would really be afraid that I might do something to hurt her. Finally, one day I admitted to my mother that sometimes I honestly felt as if I could put my daughter down by the side of the road, go off and leave her, really not caring whether someone picked her up or not. I felt horribly guilty about feeling as I did and even more so when I'd confessed — although my mother was the only person to whom I could have done so at the time. Mother chuckled and replied, "Don't think for a moment that it's because Kathy is cerebral palsied that you feel like this. At one time or another, every mother feels the same way about her children. It is just all part of being a parent, and the frustration our children can drive us to. The important thing is that you didn't put her down and leave her."

Her reassurance that I was only "normal" dispelled my own self-doubts and I could then relax and search for the solution. I could talk to Kathy's doctor in a more reasonable manner, and together we were able to find a solution. Three sons and several years later, I understood exactly what my mother had meant. There is nothing shameful about our momentary emotional reactions, our brief bursts of despair-driven anger — if we do not put these thoughts into action, and if we do not let ourselves dwell on our darker thoughts.

Let's look at my example a little more closely and deeply. Why did I feel rejection toward my small daughter? I was frustrated because I could do nothing to help her, nothing to relieve whatever distress was making her cry. My expressions of love toward her were rejected, and so I became more frustrated. Also, because my love was rejected by her, I began to dislike her because she'd hurt my feelings. I doubt that anyone who has not had the experience of being the parent of a handicapped child can fully comprehend the terrific degree of frustration which these parents go through. Frustration is always with us; it haunts us, makes us fearful of the future, and underlies all our emotional reactions. Frustration at not knowing what to do undermines our assurance that we are capable of being competent parents, and sometimes even that we can be competent people. Since there is seldom any way to determine the eventual potentiality of a child who has a deficiency in ability, the parents are quite naturally frustrated by not knowing how to plan for the future. Sometimes these frustrations mount up and overwhelm the parents until the effort to rise above their burdens seems to be just too much. It is easier then to push the child away from concern and thought for a while. But, there is still something deep inside that will not let us do that with a completely free conscience, some twinge of our heart that reminds us still of our love for this child.

Some theories of human behavior advocate that parental rejection of a handicapped child is a form of punishment directed toward the child by the parent. Perhaps, but I would place the punishment syndrome under the hostility reaction, because by the time parents have reached the reaction stage of rejection, they have usually solved those problems that most often cause hostility and have laid their guilt to rest. Parental rejection of a handicapped child derives more from fear of their own incompetence than from a desire to punish the child. The child is no longer the enemy, but rather his lack of ability is the cause of insurmountable problems. The future looks dark, and there is the ever-present fear that they are not doing enough to help their child, or that what is being done is not right. With these thoughts and with little hope that the situation will ever improve, the object that is causing the distress is pushed away so the soul can survive.

The remedy? While there is no one-step formula, there is a basic rule: look beneath the handicapping deficiency and see the child. He is first and foremost a person; the handicap is part of him, of course, but behind those eyes that do not see, the mind that doesn't learn so quickly, the lame legs, is the child himself. He is a complete personality — he is a person. He is your child, and you love him.

Strangely, perhaps, that very love parents feel for a handicapped child can also be responsible for their rejection of him and of the reality of his handicapping condition. Concern about the problems his deficiency creates for him, the life pattern he must follow because of his handicap, and all that he is denied, may cause them more pain than they can bear. Rejection of him becomes their defense against their pain. The parents' rejection would probably not be conscious, but an unconscious attitude of objectivity by which emphasis is concentrated on the handicap, with less awareness of the child himself as a person who needs their understanding and love.

Feel free to love your child and to sympathize with him — but try not to pity him.

Rejection-prompted Action

But how to recognize rejection when it is subtle and hidden behind other emotions? Understanding the cause of your feelings opens the way to understanding the motivation for the act, and understanding is nine-tenths the battle.

For some parents, their battle against rejection begins at the beginning, when the child is a very young infant at the time they are told that he suffers from deficiencies that will prevent his being considered "normal." If the handicap is physical, such as a harelip and cleft palate, a deformed or missing arm or leg, or other obvious malformations, it is natural that the parents feel some degree of rejection — they did not produce a perfect child. Although assured by the doctors that corrective measures will in time correct the condition, for a while they will have a child who is noticeably imperfect and of whom they are ashamed. In other instances, such as spina bifida or heart conditions, the parents are faced with expensive corrective surgery and a long recuperative period during which they receive no assurance that their child will recover or to what extent his abilities will develop.

The infant may be so badly damaged that the doctors advise the parents, "Place this child in an institution now, before you've learned to love him. He will never develop normally, his ability is so limited that he will always be a burden to you. It is best that you forget you ever had him and concentrate on your other children or the children you will have."

Objectively, perhaps the doctors are correct in advising some parents to follow this course of action, but most parents must know and understand that this action is best for the *child,* or else they will always feel the pains of guilt because they failed to be good parents to this child who needed them so much. However, sometimes parents must realize that this is the very best that they can do for their child. There are many instances when the infant needs the kind of treatment and the facilities that are only available in a hospital or similar type of institution. There are times when parents cannot possibly provide adequate care for their child — when the infant is hydrocephalic (water-head), for example, only in a hospital or an institution which is equipped with the machines necessary for treatment and has trained personnel can the needed therapy be obtained. There are instances when the physical health of the mother prevents her giving the extra care and attention which are required. Each family situation must be viewed separately and all aspects considered with the full recognition that sometimes parents can show more love and responsibility for their child by placing him in an institution (I despise that word, but no other will do here, so please be open-minded) than they would by keeping him at home. There is no certainty that the decision is the right one, but if the parents make a sincere effort to put their child and his needs before their own desires, they can then rest assured that they made the best decision they were capable of making at the time. And, in the final analysis, that is all we as human beings can expect to do. ("Institutionalization" is discussed at greater length in the chapter "Planning for the Future.")

When the handicapped child is at home within the family circle, rejection must still be guarded against. Rejection in this type of situation is hard to detect, because the manifestations are usually subtle and often masquerade in the disguise of concern and good care. For example, a child's physical needs may be taken care of but his emotional needs ignored. A mother may take expert care of her child and yet give little loving affection to him. Or, the father may never forget to kiss his child good night, may even help to dress him and regularly help with his exercises, but still do all with an attitude of detachment and duty rather than with a feeling of love which is freely expressed to his child. Cuddling, caressing, just loving your handicapped child is very important. Studies conducted in hospitals and orphanages have shown that babies and children need "mothering" just as much as they need food and medical treatment. Children in overcrowded institutions, where there was no time for affection, have been known to suffer mysterious ailments or to be diagnosed as mentally retarded, and yet when placed in an atmosphere where there was a "mother" to cuddle and love them, they were found to be suffering only from the lack of love.

On the other hand, parents, especially mothers, may reject their child by ignoring his physical needs. Many deficient-inability children are not demanding and seem content to lie quietly and able to entertain themselves, requiring little attention. It's very easy for a busy mother to ignore an undemanding child — the creaking door gets the oil; the crying baby gets attention. Sometimes a mother must consciously make herself aware that it is time for the baby (or child) to be fed, or changed, or otherwise taken care of because he may not be able to tell her.

Especially when a child is older, it is easy to fall into the habit of providing all the necessary or prescribed therapy and medication, but because time left over is sparse, time for loving is not in the schedule. Or, parents may provide toys and all sorts of paraphernalia for their child's therapy and improvement, even to employing someone either to help with the housework or to care for the child, and then overlook what he needs most — their expression of love for him. It is difficult to find the time to love a handicapped child — so much time must be spent in traveling back and forth to the clinic or treatment center, so many hours are spent each day doing the home exercises, teaching, and just caring for the child who is not independent. "There just aren't enough hours in the day for me to do everything I have to do!" is an often heard lament from mothers. "How can I find the time to 'show love' to my child?" But you don't have to set aside X number of minutes, or write down on your daily schedule a "loving time" — you accomplish this by your attitude and in the little things you do. How much time does it take to give your child a quick hug and kiss? How much time does it take for you to say "I love you"? A smile actually takes less energy than a frown; to think negatively is much more wearying than to think positively. Showing love is a matter of attitude, not time. Think "I love you" rather than "Why did this happen to me?" and you will show your child that you love him.

Another manifestation of rejection, especially when the child is older, is to exclude him from the family activities. Because of a physical deficiency, he may not be able to participate, or else it is extremely difficult and troublesome for his parents to take him. Or, because of a lack of mental ability, a child may cause embarrassment in social or outside-the-home situations. But remember that a handicapped child needs family-centered activities just as much as any other child does. (The handicapped child usually needs more proof that he is a part of his family, because the security of being accepted by his family is of such paramount importance to him.) The other children in the family also benefit by knowing that their handicapped sibling is considered a full-fledged member of their family by their parents — acceptance of him strengthens their feeling of security that they, too, are loved.

Now, of course, your handicapped child will be unable to participate in many types of activities, and it would be exceedingly unfair to the other children to deny them the opportunity by insisting that he always be included, but you can alter the pattern of family recreation so that sometimes you tailor-make activities in which the entire family can participate. For example, although your wheelchair bound youngster cannot play baseball, he should have the opportunity to watch his brother play and to cheer him on (he may become so interested in the game that through study and observation, he might become an excellent bench-coach). Family picnics in a park, a ride in the country to enjoy the spring flowers or fall foliage, or even a backyard picnic are types of family activities in which all members can participate.

Where you live will, of course, determine to a great extent the activities you can find, but even in a city there are parks to picnic in, circuses still travel to the medium-sized and smaller cities. Blind children can enjoy a musical concert even more sometimes than sighted people; deaf children appreciate the interplay of colors and design to be found in an art gallery or museum, and while mentally deficient children may not understand all the significance of what they see there, they benefit from and enjoy what they can understand. Zoos, whether large or small, are available to most families, and because of the variety of things to see, such an outing is an enjoyable and valuable learning experience for all the family. Gardening, whether a full-sized vegetable or flower garden or only a few pots on the window sill, provides many hours of enjoyment, and by giving the handicapped child an opportunity to contribute something to the family, helps to make him feel he is a worthwhile member.

Social adjustment is extremely important for handicapped children and a part of their training which often is most difficult for parents to provide. Regardless of the type or the extent of his handicapping deficiency, your child must learn to live in a world that is geared for the nonhandicapped. At best it is hard for a handicapped child to become a part of that world outside his home; if he feels rejected by his parents, his adjustment is well nigh impossible. There are ways, however, to help him become a part of society, and when you accomplish this you will find that much of the reason for which you reject him is overcome by your pleasure in seeing him happy. Also, because he will learn how to conduct himself in public situations, you will be less hesitant to take him out with you.

Sometimes you must find ways of adapting the socialization to suit your child's ability and particular needs; sometimes by looking around and asking, you will discover activities which have already been organized by other parents. In my community there is a bowling league for handicapped children. Some teams are made up of those who are mentally retarded, members of other teams are physically handicapped, and still others include youngsters who have multiple handicaps, such as cerebral palsy. The type of handicap makes little or no difference to these young people, for they are all members of that very special group who are handicapped. You should see how they play and the fun they have! Some are wheelchair bound, others balance on one crutch instead of the usually necessary two, some have an unsteady gait and hands that usually do not respond to command, but have learned to grasp a bowling ball and send it racing down the alley to knock down the pins. Some cannot add their scores, but someone else on the team is there to do this for them as unobtrusively as another child opens the door for a child on crutches or pushes the boy in a wheelchair up the ramp.

Did you know that basketball can be played from a wheelchair? That deaf children can play and enjoy games such as basketball and baseball and football? If there are no such special teams in your area or neighborhood, get to work and organize one. Boys and girls don't have to have a league and compete against other teams, they can enjoy playing a game just for the sheer pleasure of playing.

The Scouts have special programs for handicapped children — both boys and girls, physically handicapped and mentally retarded. There may be such a troop in your community, and if there isn't, perhaps you can organize one. Every community has resources that are untapped. One of our local churches donates the use of the parish hall one Friday night each month for dances sponsored by the local mentally retarded children's parents' organization. These parents realized that their children needed this type of activity for the development of their social adjustment. But bowling alleys and dance halls and basketball courts aren't necessary; the same results can be attained in homes to give the participants a sense of belonging to a group with whom they can compete on an equal level.

For the hyperactive, kinesthetically handicapped child, there is no better therapy than sports. Golf is also excellent therapy for the hyperactive child, and playing with his father provides a perfect opportunity for their companionable relationship. (There are off-hours when even the most crowded golf courses are nearly deserted. One father I know put a six-hole miniature golf course in the back yard of his small city lot.) Croquet is also another outdoor game that is good therapy, especially for eye-hand coordination training. If you have no yard, the children's plastic bowling sets are made to use in the house, or plastic detergent bottles and a rubber ball can be used.

As you learn how to find ways of providing pleasurable activities for your child, you will then discover that you are enjoying him more. When you can accept his limitations, then you will be able to plan family activities that also include him at times. When you learn to focus your concern on the child, you will understand and that his handicapping lack of ability is responsible for what you reject in him. If you learn to appreciate your child for what he is, rather than disliking him for what he is not, you will then be able to express your love to him. When he is confident that he is loved, then he will be able to express his own love for you.

The Whys of Rejection

Now that rejection has been examined as to what it is and how to recognize and offset rejection-caused action, let's look at some of the major causes of rejection.

Shame Although shame is usually one of the less important emotional reactions experienced by parents during the acceptance period, it is still present in some guise and to some extent all during the time they are learning to accept the reality of their child's handicapping condition. Because a feeling of shame can have a great bearing on how well they are able to adjust their attitude and life pattern to this fact, it is important to understand just what "shame" means.

According to *The American Heritage Dictionary* shame is: "a painful emotion caused by a strong sense of guilt, embarrassment, unworthiness, or disgrace; a person or thing which brings dishonor, disgrace, or condemnation." "A painful emotion caused by a strong sense of guilt" implies that the parents have been the cause of their child's disability and that his being handicapped signifies disgrace or condemnation for some weakness or misdeed they committed in the past.

This particular interpretation of shame is more often found during the earlier blame stage of acceptance; shame at the rejection stage is more often felt as embarrassment because of the attention the child attracts in public. While parents are not blamed today in the public's mind for a child's handicap, the actions of any child reflect his parents and how they have upheld their responsibilities of training him.

Embarrassment — that ill-at-ease feeling of being ashamed of the way one's child attracts attention. The mother of the hyperactive boy who is racing about the store imagines that other people are thinking, "Why doesn't she make that child behave? What he needs right now is a good spanking!" The parents of the cerebral palsied child who cannot manage a fork or spoon well and cannot control his tongue and lip muscles well enough to prevent food from dribbling down his chin, imagine the other diners in the restaurant to be saying, "Why didn't they leave that kid at home? His messiness is disgusting." And so fear of being embarrassed by their child keeps the parents from taking him outside the house, and eventually, perhaps, causes them to conceal his handicap or even his existence. Then, because they blame the child for hampering their own social life, the parents begin to resent him, and their resentment leads to rejection.

But you cannot keep your child hidden away from inquisitive or critical eyes; you must expose him to the world of people, for it is in this world he will have to learn to live and these non-handicapped people to whom he will have to learn to adapt himself. Much of the attitude of other people toward your handicapped child depends upon your own attitude and how you treat your child and his mishaps and misbehavior. If you treat him with warm, calm understanding, so will other people treat him; if you react with angry dislike and obvious embarrassment, so will the audience react.

One day my husband and I took our three sons into an ice cream shop, crowded with little boys celebrating their victory at a Little League baseball game. Also waiting to be served was a young couple with their little daughter. All of a sudden, this little flaxen-haired, five-year-old angel turned into a whirling-dervish imp, racing about the store and jabbering loudly in a nonsense language. There was little indication from her appearance that she had any problem except the lack of discipline, but it soon became apparent to us that her hyperactivity was only a part of whatever her particular handicap was. We were all shocked into silence and acutely embarrassed for ourselves and for the little girl's parents. Then her father calmly and quietly picked her up and held her close to him until she quieted. There were no stern commands of "Be quiet!" or "Behave yourself!"; no spanking or other discipline. The line was long, and the wait must have been intolerably long for the little girl, for a few minutes later, she burst out into the same sort of behavior. Her mother responded in a manner similar to that used by her father earlier. This time, the spectators paid little or no attention to the child or to the parents — the calm and assured manner in which her parents handled her had put us all at ease because we were not embarrassed for the parents, or for ourselves.

So take your clue from this example. That mother and father did not care what the rest of us thought about their daughter's behavior, or what we thought of them and their capability to handle her, or even if we criticized them for bringing her into the shop where she could not follow the pattern of acceptable behavior. Their concern was obviously for their daughter and how best to help her adjust to the surroundings. (From experience, I'm quite sure the parents were *very* aware of the reactions of the other people. They were, no doubt, wondering why in the world they'd ever dared bring her there at all!) We all sympathized with the parents, but it was not pity that we felt for them, rather it was admiration. "They'll make it all right," my husband summarized. I have no doubt that they will, for they obviously have learned to listen to their hearts, not to the criticisms of an unknowledgeable audience.

Society's reaction to the child is an important factor in parental rejection, for within the home the parents can adjust to and accept most types of bizarre behavior. It is when the eye of the public is focused on the child that the family feels the sharpness of censure which causes their embarrassment. However, even within the privacy of the home, there are other reasons which lead to parental rejection of the child because of shame. Some handicapped children are, quite frankly, unpleasant to be around — the older child who constantly drools, or one who lacks bladder or bowel control, or a child whose facial features are distorted or whose body is so malformed as to be grotesque. Rejection then is an easy course of action to follow because — let's admit the truth — overlooking these aspects of the handicap is hard to do, even by the most loving parents. If yours is a similar situation, there are ways of coping, measures you can take to lessen the problem. For the child who cannot control his toilet needs, there are now disposable diapers, which also contain a built-in deodorant, and other "diapers" and covers designed especially for the older child or adult who is incontinent. Check with a hospital supply company if you cannot find these items, or even with the local hospital. While there are no devices I know about to control or conceal drooling, there are measures which can be taken to make this less noticeable and therefore less of a source for your embarrassment. One of the most important measures is keeping the child clean — far better to have more inexpensive clothes and change them frequently than to have a few "nice" outfits. If drooling is one of your child's problems, as it is our Kathy's, make small drool-bibs to match or complement dresses or blouses — and since boys also have this problem, drool-bibs can be made to complement their shirts. While these certainly do not alleviate the drooling, at least it is less noticeable.

Parental shame due to a child's lack of accomplishment is also a very important factor in rejection. It is, in a way, a summation of all the other causes, for in our society which places such high value on success, often it is difficult to reconcile oneself to having a child who is unable to be "a success." It is with children who are deficient in mental ability that parents feel most deeply a sense of being ashamed of their child because of his lack of achievement. "If only he had normal intelligence, I could overlook his physical handicap," a parent often feels. There is a mysteriousness, a wariness, when a child cannot think and reason and learn, and here again the parents set the tone of his acceptance by others by their own attitude. If it is one of calm, matter-of-fact acceptance of his lack of ability, of accentuating his positive attributes, so will others look upon the mentally retarded or brain-injured child.

"My child is mentally retarded — what can he do, even though he is physically strong?" There are many ways for the mentally retarded to use their talents and abilities, even many jobs that are opening up now in which a less mentally endowed person can perform better, such as certain types of routine tasks so necessary in industry. Nursery school personnel are discovering that trained mentally retarded people make excellent teachers' aides, especially for the younger children. Gardening, animal care, many types of service-oriented jobs are other areas in which people classified as "slow learners" and even "educable" are working successfully. There are now many avenues open by which a mentally retarded person can find ways to add dignity and purpose to his life.

When a child is handicapped only by a physical deficiency, almost any compensating achievement he accomplishes is lauded, and he and his parents are praised for his success. That is good, and as it should be, but parents of these children also must temper their urging, lest overcoming the handicap — or proving that success can be accomplished in spite of the handicap — becomes more important than the child. If your child's handicap is physical, be careful that you do not sacrifice acceptance of the person your child is by striving to have him reach goals of achievement. Without the security of knowing his parents love and accept him for what he is, his achievement will be won at the cost of his personal happiness and self-esteem. Encourage him to reach toward the outer limits of his ability, but don't let your disappointment in his failures show too much, or he may interpret your disappointment as disappointment *in* him rather than *for* him.

Resentment Parental resentment of the extra burdens they must carry because their child is handicapped is a logical cause of rejection. The financial burden is perhaps the heaviest, for most parents are able to meet the cost of the medical care, treatment and therapy, special training for their handicapped child only by sacrifice and self-denial. Also, caring for such a child can be a tremendous drain on the mother's physical energy, time, and emotional well-being. If there are other children in the family, usually they also must make sacrifices of material possessions and of their parents' time and concern.

It's only natural for parents to resent their children at times — even parents of normal children sometimes feel overloaded by the burdens of parental responsibility and child demands. But for them these responsibilities will end in a few years, the demands are spasmodic and of short duration; for those parents whose children are handicapped, the duration of their responsibilities may be life-long, the demands constant and difficult to meet, the need for sacrifice and self-denial never-ending. Therefore, their resentment must be counteracted, because if allowed to grow both child and parent will be harmed.

The time to begin resolving any resentment you may feel toward your child is at the beginning of your awareness that he is handicapped. Look at him and see him as the unique person he is, not as a reflection of what you are. Realize that your primary role in his life is to teach him how to be happy — that is your basic responsibility to him. Everything parents do for their children is directed toward this goal — the discipline, all the various areas of knowledge attainment, even nourishing their bodies. But all your efforts will be in vain, if your child does not know you love him and that you are happy because of him. So laugh with your child, and he will laugh with you; love him, and he will return your love a thousandfold; find something in him to be proud of, and he will glow with happiness. Children are not mirror images of their parents, but they do reflect how their parents feel toward them.

Now, on to a more practical, workable, everyday solution to resentment. Don't let yourself become a martyr to your child and his needs and demands. You must find time for yourself; you must find ways to give yourself something for which you feel a gratified sense of accomplishment. Look back to the chapter, "Withdrawal," and refresh your memory of some of the mechanics of finding time for yourself. While your child is busy at the clinic or in school, do something you want to do and cannot with him along.

One of the best ways to shake off resentment is to do something for someone else. There are so many people who need thoughtfulness from someone, and often it is neither a matter of money nor time — just a small reminder that they are not forgotten, that someone cares.

Amazingly, when you become aware of the problems other

people have, you will begin to realize that yours just may not be so bad after all. (And as a side benefit, the satisfaction you derive from helping someone else and knowing you are useful will also help you accept yourself and the worthwhileness of your own talents and abilities.)

As long as your outside-the-home activities serve to help you feel more useful, keep up your good work, for your involvement then helps you to be a better person and a more effective parent. But, be careful — don't let other people's needs become more important to you than those of your own family, for therein lies neglect, which leads ultimately to rejection. (Seems that life is a continual effort to maintain the proper balance, doesn't it?)

If you hesitate to cut down on your involvement outside your family, because you are afraid you cannot cope with the prospect of being unable to achieve your goals at home, perhaps your goals should be reevaluated. Instead of looking toward the long-range goals you *hope* your child will reach, look instead at the short-term, everyday goals he *can* reach. Rather than dreaming of the day when your child can run, realize that the first, wobbly step he takes with the aid of the walking-bars or crutches is a major victory. Don't pin your hopes and dreams on the day when your child may enter college; accept as a major goal his learning to read the traffic sign that tells him to STOP. Let the first time she sets the table with no mistakes be a day of celebration; the day your child says, "I love you" and you understand the words, be a time for joy. In other words, look at the everyday, small accomplishments, and let these be victories and milestones of accomplishment and progress.

Fear and the Burdensome Future   Fear is another reason for parental rejection of a handicapped child, less obvious but no less valid.

Fear is a constant companion to parents whose children are handicapped. It is present from the very beginning, when they are afraid their child will not recover from the illness or that the tests will prove the damage to be beyond repair. It crops up over and over again during all the stages of acceptance, but not until this last stage has been reached does fear become really important and consistent. Up until this time when all evidence begins to crystallize into reality, the parents have been comforted by the hope that their child will not be permanently handicapped — that a cure will be found or that he will "outgrow" his difficulties. Hope and fear cannot live together in the same heart, so when hope is finally defeated, fear is waiting to take over.

Like grief, fear is most often short-lived at its worst intensity (panic) and transitory at its best; but it can be as destructive as any of the other negative emotional reactions. Because it can cause an impenetrable wall to grow around the heart through which love cannot pass, fear can be a major contributing factor to parental rejection of their handicapped child. Because of his handicap, the child represents so much of the cause of his parents' uncertainty and all the unknowns that give rise to their fears.

All parents have fear concerning their children, but the fears experienced by parents of nonhandicapped children fall more into the category of vagueness, of what might happen to their child — he might be hurt playing football, driving a car, riding a motorcycle, or he might be led into trouble by undesirable companions — the reality of cause and effect, of his action and the result. The fears of parents concerning their children who are handicapped fall more into the realm of the known and are more the responsibility of the parent rather than the child. These parents already know that their lives will be different because their children are different. They don't wonder what they will do if their child is maimed, for that is already fact and reality in their lives. Basically, I suppose, the fears of all parents stem from a sense of personal inability to be a good parent — and often, confusion as to what being a "good parent" really means. But parents whose children are handicapped and therefore dependent upon them, feel this responsibility more deeply than do those whose children are capable of being independent. The parent of a handicapped child feels in a very real sense that he is responsible for two lives, and also, that he has less chance for a second try to correct his mistakes.

As parents become cognizant of the reality of their child's deficiency, they can then allow themselves to look into the future — in fact, they cannot *not* look into the future. Then, as the future unfolds in their mind's eye, that gloomy path ahead darkened by disappointment and a sense of futility, overshadowed by circumstances over which they have no control or hope of improving, they become fearful of their own strength of character and their ability to carry the burdens without faltering. Sometimes this fear grows into a magnitude of overwhelming proportions, and when the parents are thus beaten down by their fear, neither the child nor his handicapping deficiency can be accepted. Either the child is ignored and rejected, or the handicap is not accepted as being real. Many times, it is fear that motivates a parent to abandon his child.

Present always in parents' minds is the fear that they are not doing enough to improve the child's condition, or that what is being done is not the best or most effective approach. (Often this is the particular sword that mothers feel to be hanging over their heads.)

For a father, especially, there is the fear of not being able to provide enough financial security for his child who will be unable to be independent. While parents of nonhandicapped children also worry about being able to provide financial security for their children, there is still the reassuring thought in the back of their minds that their children could make it on their own if necessary. The father of a handicapped child has no such reassurance. On the contrary, he knows that his child could *not* take care of himself or his financial needs; because of either a physical or a mental lack of ability, his child will never be totally independent — at best he will be only partially independent, at worst he will be totally dependent upon someone else.

Also, both parents are fearful of the continuancy of their love for their handicapped child. "I love my child now while he is young, but will I always feel this way toward him? Will the burdens, the disappointments, eventually corrupt my love for him?" And for both parents, there is the additional fear that the problems their child's condition creates will destroy the unity of the family circle. They know his handicap is the cause of extraordinary pressures on the other children as well as on the bonds between husband and wife and fear that they will not be strong enough to withstand this strain on their lives. Will they be able to give continuously of themselves, despite receiving so little in return from this child?

Only a limited scope of fear can be discussed here, because each person has his own particular fear-imps determined by his personality and the type and degree of severity of his child's handicap. Still, there are certain overall approaches to conquering fear which are applicable to all.

First, learn to live each day for itself. Let yesterday's problems remain in the past, and don't worry about what tomorrow's problems might be. Not worrying about tomorrow's problems doesn't mean that you should not make preparations for the future. If the indications are that your child will be dependent or even semidependent, you must make some plans and preparations for his care in the future, for your responsibility for him extends beyond today, and even, perhaps, beyond your own life span. You will find a great sense of relief from fear when you make some sort of provision for your child's future financial security and care.

None of us ever has complete faith or confidence in our own decision-making ability, and those who say they do are only trying to fool themselves and others. But, on the other hand, by accepting the fact that all you can do is to make the best decisions you are capable of making at the time in the light of what you know then, you will free yourself of much unnecessary fear. Don't make blind, hasty decisions, of course; investigate, study, talk to other people who might help you. Then, have faith in your own ability and strength of character. When all is said and done, the final decision is up to you alone to make. Ultimately, each of us must listen to our own heart.

Just as hope and fear cannot live in the same heart, neither can faith in God and fear reside side by side in the same mind. The very best ammunition with which to fight fear is faith in the Lord. Trusting in Him, believing that He will guide and strengthen, how then can we fear anything?

Among other fears that plague parents of handicapped children is fear that they will not be able to cope with their disappointment of being denied the pleasures of parenthood they had anticipated. But don't be afraid — you will find the strength to overcome your disappointment. Once you accept your child as he is, not as you wish he were, your anticipations will not be so important.

Refuse to let fear rule, and you will be able to give your child what he needs most — your love. Through your freely expressed love of him, he will develop that all-important sense of security of knowing you accept him as the person he is inside those deficiencies which handicap him and make him different from other children. He will know then that he is important, that he is not rejected by those who are the most important people in his world — his mother and father.

When a child feels that his parents have rejected him, there may be a backlash — he may fight back by rejecting his parents (or the parent who he feels rejects him). There is little so frustrating and demoralizing to a parent as finding that a child does not accept advances of affection. Sometimes the backlash is of a different character, such as when the child uses his lack of ability as a means of getting the love and attention he feels he is being denied from his parents. He may play up his handicapping lack of ability — the "Poor Me" syndrome, forcing his dependence upon his parents and refusing to make the effort to learn to develop the skills that could lead to his being more independent. Or, a child may use his handicap as a means of maneuvering his parents, perhaps even playing one against the other, into overindulging his whims and wants. No child should have the upper hand with his parents, yet this is exactly what can happen when a child is rejected, because a child must have his parents' attention, even if he has to achieve this through negative attempts.

Summary

Although some feeling of rejection is present in the parents' relationship with their child from the very beginning of the realization that "something is wrong," it is not until they are faced with the undeniable permanence of their child's lack of ability that rejection becomes a major road block to their acceptance of the reality of the handicapping condition. Most often rejection is prompted by a last effort to regain hope, a last attempt not to submit to the inevitable, and a fight against the fear that now threatens.

Knowledge will be your best weapon against rejection and fear, for knowledge will provide understanding, and understanding will enable you to find and develop the strength that you possess within yourself.

Knowing and understanding the limits of your child's ability will help you find ways in which you can develop what potential he has and will help you keep your expectation level within realistic and reasonable boundaries. When you learn to overlook what you had expected to find in a child, you will be able to see this child as the unique person he is. When you learn to lay aside your early hopes and dreams and think of him, then you will hear what your heart is saying.

7. Acceptance: Destination Reached

WITH REJECTION OVERCOME, your progress along the road to acceptance will be complete. You will be able to say, "My child is handicapped," and believe that what you say is true.

This journey to Acceptance is not easy for you, nor is it for anyone. Stumbling over the emotional reactions that block the way is often painful, but each time you overcome a danger of defeat you grow in strength and gain courage through conviction in your capability to cope with whatever adversity you may encounter in the future.

As you learn that your child will never be as able as other children or as the child you had anticipated, you learn to accept the limitations of his ability — not only the lowest, but the possibility of the highest. As you learn to accept him as he is, not as the child you wish he were, you can then look beneath his handicapping deficiencies and see the person he is — not a handicapped-child, but as a child who is handicapped.

You learn much about yourself as you progress along this road, for acceptance is also accepting yourself as you are, acknowledging your weaknesses and recognizing your strengths. You learn, too, that grief does not last forever; life does go on and the sun is behind the clouds. As you struggle to absolve yourself of guilt, you realize that regardless of who may have been responsible for this having happened to your child, being concerned with placing the blame is useless — what is past is past, and your concern is with the future.

Some roadblocks will stand out in the brightness of victory, while others may remain covered with the gloom of failure. But there is no reason to feel remorse because of what you believe were your failures — through defeat you learn how to prevent other mistakes and build the strength you need to continue your progress.

And, you will learn much of which you may not yet be aware. You will learn to recognize and appreciate the goodness that life has to offer because you have known so much despair and pain. Since you face so many big problems, you will learn to take the little problems in stride and how to better differentiate between those that are small and unimportant and those that are worth being concerned about. You learn the importance of asking for help and of accepting help when it is offered. You will learn, too, that not all advice is good, that you must consider, ponder, and then make up your own mind as to the best course of action. Perhaps most important, you will learn to listen to your heart because you will have more faith in your own ability and judgment.

Because you have been face-to-face with human frailties, you will grow in your capacity to feel compassion for others and in your understanding and acceptance of people as they are. You will recognize how much good is inherent in people and know something of the cruelty that possesses others. Because you learn to go beyond the limits of your own needs and desires, you will become more aware of the needs of others and of your responsibility to help when you can. And in fulfilling your responsibilities to others, you will know the gratification of being a whole person.

You have known the destruction of some of your hopes and dreams, but you know that the future holds promise of other hopes, other dreams. It is on these altered sets of values that you now adjust your sights.

PART II

ADJUSTMENT

ADJUSTMENT IS WHAT it is all about; the end toward which you work. In essence, adjustment is how you manage your life now that this situation has been forced upon you; how you are going to rephase your life pattern so the necessary new goals and ambitions can be encompassed in your planning. Basically, the decision is up to you alone to make. Are you going to give up and be defeated, or are you going to take up the challenge and channel the effects of this circumstance into something good and worthwhile?

You bet it's a big job and the going will get awfully rough at times! There will be those times when you will wish you could hide in a corner and tell the rest of the world to go away and leave you alone. There will be other times when you will wish you could run away and begin a new life, because your burdens are so heavy in this one. You know you cannot actually run away. Truthfully, you do not really want to do so — you simply want to know how to manage. How can you become strong enough to meet the challenges and carry the burdens? How can you gather together the good that has survived this catastrophe and with that build some kind of worthwhile life for yourself and your child?

The answer? You adjust. And the adjustment begins with yourself — how you think and how you feel deep inside the unique personality that is your true self.

Before one can begin to adjust, one must first understand what this means. Again, let us turn to the dictionary definition for help. In the *Little Oxford Dictionary of Current English*

(Fourth Edition. Compiled by George Ostler, edited by Jessie Coulson. Great Britain: Oxford University Press, 1969) the verb adjust is defined as: "to arrange, to put in order, to harmonize, to adapt." In *The American Heritage Dictionary,* adjust is: "to change so as to fit; to bring into proper relationship; to adapt or to conform, as to new conditions." From the *World Book Dictionary*: "adjust emphasizes the idea of matching one thing to another; adapt emphasizes the idea of making minor changes in a thing (or a person)." Also from the *World Book Dictionary*: "adjustment (psychology): the process by which a person adapts himself to the natural or social conditions around him." Therefore, by definition, to adjust implies action. It is action taken *by* the person, not action that is done to or for him by others. It is a positive action in that it is a moving forward, not a negative one or a standing still and slipping backward.

Actually, in the very simplest sense of the meaning, adjustment is living. Life is a constant series of changes, of altering plans to meet the demands of new situations, of modifying hopes and ambitions when circumstances or events precipitate a redirection of goals.

Adjustment is not a stage that abruptly begins on the day you learn to accept the reality of your child's lack of ability. You began adjusting the day you were first aware that "something is wrong" — that your child's development was slower than that of the other children his age, or when you began to doubt whether he would fully recover from the illness or be completely rehabilitated after the accident. Nor is adjustment a battle that is ever completely finished, for it will continue the rest of your life, just as you have been engaged in this fight all along the road to Acceptance. "Battle" and "fight" are appropriate words to use in talking about adjustment, because that is exactly the way you will feel many times as you struggle against depression, disappointment, guilt, decision making, and a frustrating confusion of other problems. It will seem to reach almost overwhelming proportions at times.

Now that you are somewhat prepared for the dark side of the reality of adjustment, let me assure you that the future is not all dismal and bleak. There will be many instances of joy, and because you have known so much disappointment and un-happiness, you will appreciate the good days and the happy times with a greater intensity and depth than do most people. As time passes, the moods of depression, the periods of dis-appointment and frustration will become less intense, of shorter duration, and farther apart. And because you will have worked so hard to find some semblance of balance and order and pur-pose in your life, you will learn that you have strengthened your character in all the finer, more important aspects.

Your adjustment to this altered pattern of your life is in-fluenced by attitudes you held long before the handicap was known, even before your child was born. Much has to do with just what you expected from your role as a parent: Why did you want to be a parent? Was the child wanted? Can you let go of your vision of the perfect child easily? How strong are the reasons that hold you back from doing so? The manner in which you cope with the various problems of your adjustment is determined to a great extent by the kind of person you are. How well do you handle disappointments? How strong a fighter are you? How willing are you to seek out solutions to the problems and then to follow through on what you've learned? All these are questions that you must ask yourself and then learn to use the answers as your weapons and tools.

There is nothing easy about adjustment. You are not dealing now with minor, insignificant changes or surface feelings — you are having to look hard and deep into the very core of your personality, to search for a "gut-level" insight that will enable you to understand what makes you tick. Don't expect this insight to come suddenly — personality is complex and many faceted. Most often you will make only small chips in the armor that surrounds your ego, although at times a sudden gleam of insight will reveal a particular facet for your under-standing. Adjustment is a life-long process, not only because it takes time to really know yourself (and some people never do), but because as new circumstances occur, you must learn to harmonize your reactions so you can arrange these new conditions in the proper relationship.

All this may sound like a big order and an overwhelming prospect of the future. In many aspects this is true, for regardless of the type or the extent of your child's handicapping deficiency, you are going to have to change, and change is always difficult. But this change doesn't have to be made overnight — and cannot be, in fact — you proceed one step at a time, day by day.

Remember this and be consoled — you are not alone: there are many people and many sources of help for you. Most important, you are much more capable than you realize. You have already taken the most important step forward by accepting the reality of the existence of your child's handicap. In comparison to what you have been through in reaching this victory, the rest of the way is downhill progress.

So look up now and see all the good that is in your life. Count your many blessings. This is not the end of your world; it is the beginning of another which can be more meaningful because you will be able to appreciate all the riches you will earn.

Adjustment may be difficult, but it will become less so as time passes. As you pass each milestone, reaching the next one is easier. You doubt the possibility for real happiness now? Nonsense! There is plenty of happiness ahead for you. But you must look up so you can recognize happiness — if you keep your eyes focused on the troubled ground, you will pass right by happiness without even knowing it is here. If you allow the bricks of disappointment to be cemented by your self-pity, you will only build a soundproof wall around your heart.

While much of adjustment has to do with emotion and personality, there is also need for action. There are short cuts which will make it easier for you; there are methods and courses of action which will help you help yourself. We learn by doing, but we also can learn by knowing what others in similar situations have done. Because your child is handicapped, he has unusual problems which you as his parent must help him solve; sometimes you must solve his problems for him, just as you would if he were not handicapped. In the following chapters, ways of solving the problems are suggested. Perhaps you will think some of the methods or problems do not apply to your particular situation, but you will often find that you can profit from the experiences others have been through by gaining a clearer insight into your own problems.

Up until the time you reach Acceptance, your adjustment has been subtle, for not until you know your child's handicap is a permanent condition do you recognize the need to adjust your life pattern to fit this altered situation. Until now, you have been adapting, now you will begin adjusting.

1. The Search for Solutions

YOU HAVE NOW accepted the reality of your child's lack of ability, and you know that the permanence of his handicap is a certainty. What will your next step be? Where do you go from here?

When the full realization hits, you cry awhile again over your loss. Again you are assailed by fears of the future and doubtful of your ability to cope with whatever problems may be in store for you. But then the tears must be dried, and your fears somehow put aside, for you have plans to make and a course of action to chart. Probably you feel lost and confused now, almost as if you are standing on a wave-buffeted beach looking out at the rough, uncharted sea over which you must cross to reach the distant, fog-shrouded shore. You need help, because the tide is rising fast, and you feel so alone.

There is, however, a bright glow in this dark scene — you have been relieved of the frustration of not knowing. No longer need you be plagued by the thought that somewhere there is someone who holds the key that will unlock the door to the cure for your child's blindness, or deafness, or mental retardation, or whatever his deficiency may be — if you only could find that person. Instead of vague dreams and unreachable goals, you now have a definite foundation upon which to begin adjusting the pattern of your life.

This new attitude is not one of hopelessness and defeat — there is still plenty of room for hope, only now the goals toward which your hope is directed are altered. Rather than hoping your child will one day be as other children are, your hopes for your child now are directed toward his being happy. It is to this end that you direct your efforts now. Think about this and don't be surprised to learn you have to look deep into your heart to see beneath that which you had once hoped to gain *from* your child.

Ah, but you cannot just sit back now and say, "It is done; there is no need for further training or more therapy." No, to see your hopes come true you must still seek solutions, but now the solutions you seek will be for the way to best help your child develop the ability that he does have.

"Best help" means just that — the plan which most suits his needs when all aspects are considered, such as his degree and type of deficiency, his talents and projected potential, even the family situation as to finances and other children. Also, the locality in which you live influences the plans you make — the availability of facilities for his training and therapy, and the cost and transportation. All these aspects must be weighed and balanced against each other.

In order to help your child, you must formulate a plan of action, and to do this, you need information which you can obtain from various sources. Once you know how to begin your search for information, you will discover there are many sources and many people to open the door.

Gaining a Clearer Picture of the Handicap

You have been given bits and pieces of information about your child's condition by the various professional people who have examined him, and so you now have some understanding of what his handicap is all about. If you are like most parents, however, as you begin to try to formulate some plan of action, you realize you need to know much more. Or perhaps you need help in correlating all you have been told, so you can have a clearer picture of the situation. But where do you begin?

If you are among the fortunate few who have access to a

good clinic, well staffed with physicians, psychologists, and counselors who are interested in the parents and their problems, you have to look no further. All the help you need is right before you, just let your needs be known. Ask questions so you will give these people an insight into what and how much you wish to learn. Don't be hesitant, be honest.

But if you are among the vast majority of parents who have no such source of aid and counsel, you must go out in search of the answers yourself. The best source with which to begin is usually the person who told you of the definiteness of the handicap. Usually this is a physician, although it may have been a public health nurse, a social worker, or a school counselor or psychologist. Whoever the person was, he was an authority, so use the storehouse of information he knows. Talk to this person, convince him that you really do want to know.

The first kind of information you will need to know is something of the limits of your child's ability — what is reasonable for you to expect him to be able to accomplish? You have been told this before, but now you are able to listen objectively (not defensively, as you have tended to do in the past). Included in this type of information are such related issues as behavioral patterns, which will serve as a guide for the way you discipline him. What sort of achievement goals can be substituted for those that are unattainable for him? These might include concentration on intellectual pursuits if his limbs are nonfunctioning, athletic achievements if his intellectual ability is impaired, or the development of an unsuspected talent. Does his handicap indicate a short attention span and easy distractability? If so, this must be taken into consideration. Will he benefit from use of mechanical aids such as crutches or braces, hearing aid, special reading equipment? And if so, is a source of financial aid available for you? (Also, check to see if your health insurance policy includes coverage for such items.) Is corrective surgery a possibility? Again, each suggestion for helping your child overcome some degree of his handicapping condition must be considered and weighed in the light of the predicted extent of benefit and the pain, cost, and/or discomfort for him. In other words, is it worth it — or will the resulting benefit be so little that it is hardly worth the expense and the discomfort?

Sometimes we parents must say no to a suggested avenue of help for our child, and this is perhaps one of the hardest decisions we are asked to make. We do not want to deny our child anything which may make his life a little easier and happier, but still, neither do we wish to subject him to unnecessary hardship in the faint hope that he will improve because of the treatment. Also, quite frankly, the money an operation or some other type of treatment costs may be more helpful to the child if spent in other ways. Only through the knowledge you gain by talking to those who know, by benefiting from the experiences of other parents who have faced the same situation, and by having a grasp of the overall picture of your child's particular handicap, can you hope to make an intelligent decision.

Your child's doctor is your best referral source for the facilities for administration of tests which will serve as a guide in making your decisions. More than likely, he has already done so, and even perhaps referred you to a testing or diagnostic clinic. If you have not done so yet, don't hesitate any longer, because you need to know the results of a battery of profile tests. If you find your financial situation doesn't leave room for the fees of a private testing service, don't give up — there are other approaches. You may have a Family Service Agency in your community, or there may be a testing clinic sponsored by a civic organization. If you live near enough to a university or college, investigate the possibility of using their student-training testing facilities. Your public school system may also have a testing program.

If you have trouble finding literature and information about your child's handicap, write to the appropriate agency. Nearly every type of handicapping condition now has a national organ-

ization, and much of their work is devoted to providing literature to educate parents about their children's condition. These
main offices also usually have a listing of the treatment centers
in the various localities and serve as a guide for locating other
parents whose children are handicapped by a similar disability.
Government agencies, both federal and state, are a gold mine
of information. You will find addresses of offices listed in the
Appendix.

You will want to know what facilities are available in your
community for therapy and special training or education. Depending upon the type and the extent of the deficiency as well
as your child's present age, you may find that the public
school system has a program suitable for him. However, let us
hope that you've discovered your child's problem before he has
reached school age, so you can begin his special education and
training before he is eligible for the public school program.
Your doctor should know of the community resources, but if
he does not, or if he lives in another area, consult your telephone directory under "Schools, Special or Private." Public
school counseling offices are usually aware of the community
resources as are elementary school principals.

Special Training and Therapy

Once you have found out what kind of therapy and training
will benefit your child, you begin your search for the clinic,
training center, special classes or school that will best suit his
needs. Prompt enrollment is very important for your child's
development, but you will also gain many benefits.

First, because you will be doing something constructive to
help your child, you will be relieved of much of your feeling of
ineptitude. Knowing you are no longer totally responsible
for his development, that someone trained and experienced is
sharing the load of responsibility, will give you a sense of relief.
And you will benefit greatly from the opportunity to associate

with other parents who have the same type of problems that are plaguing you.

When you were trying to find out what is wrong with your child, and later, when you were struggling to accept his handicapped condition, you found solace through the sense of comradeship you felt with other parents of handicapped children when you discussed your experiences and shared your frustrations. Now that his handicap is a certainty, you will find association with these parents even more helpful as you learn how they have adjusted to the altered pattern of their lives. Much of what you will learn will be practical — how to cope with the everyday problems of family adjustment, feeding, discipline, and even toilet-training. Not the least of the many benefits you gain will be the realization of the many blessings you have — you will find you have much for which to be thankful. Some of this is repetition of what was written in Part I about the various stages of acceptance, I realize. But then you were searching for ways in which your child's performance level could be raised to that of normal; now you are concerned with the practical application of what you have learned.

"But there is nothing available here in my community," you say? If this should be so, consider starting something yourself. It has been done before. How do you think all these other school and treatment centers were begun? Talk to parents whose children need similar facilities, search out agencies — either private or governmental — which can be your funding or sponsoring agency. Don't be bashful, ask around, explore the possibilities. The more you talk about the need, the more people you will interest in filling this void. You'd be amazed to learn what can be accomplished by a very few willing people.

For example, I've watched with interest and a great deal of admiration, the development of an "opportunity center" in my small hometown. Two couples whose children are handicapped (one by mental retardation, the other by a physical disability) started the ball rolling. When they first began, they learned that neither government funds nor sponsorship by a national agency was available because there were not the required number of children with any one particular handicap in this rural community to meet the necessary quota, and so they enlisted the aid of a local service organization. This club helped in locating other children who were eligible for a special school, obtained desks and other equipment. The newspaper publicized the project, and a small house was donated. But, there were still no funds for paying the salary of a qualified teacher, even if someone could be found. Then, by a stroke of luck, they had a teacher — a young couple moved to town, and the wife was trained and experienced in special education. She agreed to teach for the small salary that could be raised through tuition and to train volunteer helpers. Less than a year after the inception of the idea of beginning a school in which their children could receive the special education and training they needed, these parents saw the freshly painted doors to their school open to admit the first class of twelve children. Several were mentally retarded, two were deaf, and another was visually handicapped, two were physically handicapped and wheelchair-bound, and another had a heart defect that prohibited his attending a regular class. Eventually a minimal fund was released from the state education department, because about half the children were of school age and the local school offered no program for them. So far, there is still only one "qualified" teacher, no physical therapist or occupational therapist, and only a part-time, visiting psychologist — but there are plenty of teacher's aides. Because of the lack of facilities and personnel, the situation is far from ideal, but everything has to have a beginning, and what is there is surely infinitely better than what was not there before.

"But these people had the support of the townspeople," you say? Of course they did, and they would not have seen the realization of their dream otherwise. But, would it have been done at all if four people had not decided to work to find a way?

(As a side note — the small house that became the school was the home of a much loved citizen who had retired after teaching some fifty years in the town. She died before the plans were completed, but in her will she had given the house to this group of parents for a school for "special" students. The school now bears her name — a very fitting memorial to someone who gave so much of herself to so many children throughout the years of her life.)

The school where our own daughter resides so happily was begun by a mother and father after they had searched unsuccessfully for a residential school for their severely handicapped son. Finding none which met their specifications, they came back home, bought a small farm, and turned the large farmhouse into a school. Today it ranks high among residential schools for handicapped children, and some of the more advanced theories of teaching and therapy are used to help the eighty resident students develop their potential in a loving atmosphere of acceptance.

Yes, I have also helped found a treatment center. The ground had already been broken by other parents when Kathy was a year old, and we moved to the small but growing town. An unused barracks on the abandoned Air Force base had been obtained, the chapter of a national organization for crippled children had been chartered, and a physical therapist had been hired from funds supplied by this organization, but there was still much to be done before the center would be ready for operation. Fathers (and some mothers, too) painted the walls, built specially designed furniture, child care was arranged so volunteer part-time teachers could offer their time, the parents' group was organized, a volunteer speech therapist was found (me!), and a child psychologist from the nearest large town was persuaded to lend his helping hand in testing and evaluating the prospective students. Eventually, our small clinic grew into a well-staffed, full-time day school, enrolling children who were handicapped by all types of deficiencies.

What does all this discussion about founding schools have to do with your adjustment? A great deal, for it illustrates what can be done when parents decided to do something about readjusting the situation to suit their needs. The world is not going to beat a path to your door to help you repattern your life. For a while, others will be interested and will try to help, but they, even those who are closest in love and friendship, will soon lose interest and sympathy if you do not respond by doing something to help yourself.

You are adjusting when you take steps to provide for your child the training that will help him develop his potential. You are adjusting your goals of achievement for your child because you are making your aspirations suit his limits of ability and his potential for the limits of his development.

Most of what has been suggested so far has involved action on your part, performing deeds and working toward a goal. But what about nonaction, contemplation so you can adjust your thinking and your emotional reactions? That is necessary, too, for thought must come before the deed. You are quite right in thinking that active participation is useless unless you have also been able to adjust your own ego to this situation. The activity serves the vital purpose of widening your perspective and directing your thinking along more logical and purposeful lines of reasoning. Until you have begun to make some plans for your child, you cannot concentrate on your own outlook upon your life.

Actually, one goes hand in hand with the other, for as you work to help your child, you are also learning how to readjust your own life.

2. Your Relationship with Your God

(Religion is not important to everyone, nor does everyone have a belief in God. Since this is directed especially to those who may feel their reactions to having a handicapped child are in conflict with basic tenets of religious teaching, readers who are not concerned with religious faith can easily skip this chapter without interruption of the continuity of the text.)

ONE ASPECT OF adjustment which cannot be coped with by action is your feeling about your God. Religion is personal, because it concerns how one feels and thinks about an abstract Supreme Being and the human relationship to Him. Deeds are important, but deeds without faith are man-directed, not God-inspired.

Your faith and your understanding of God was important all through the time you were learning to accept yor child's handicap. For some of you, much of the struggle to surmount the roadblocks was determined by how you felt about your relationship to your concept of God. Some of you found you could not reconcile your feelings of anger, guilt, disappointment, and resentment with what you believed God to be. Others of you learned to expand your understanding, and your deepened faith made acceptance possible.

Although response to concepts of religion permeates each of the stages of emotional reaction throughout the entire period of acceptance, religion has been purposely omitted from much of the previous discussion, because realistically, only when a person is ready to listen can he open his heart to hear. Until that time he is too often "turned off" and may even become antagonistic by the very mention of the words "God" or "faith." When one is struggling to understand and cope with the guilt his resentment and disappointment arouses, being reminded of how he should feel about his faith and his responsibilities toward his God often only serves to make him more guilty and therefore more resentful.

Now that the time has come for concentration on your adjustment, many of you will realize that you must also reexamine and reevaluate your relationship with God. Because faith is such an important part of the entire process of adjustment, a separate chapter is therefore devoted to discussion of the man-to-God relationship.

Regardless of how you may feel at the time you read this, I can assure you that without faith and trust in God, you will be weaker and less able to cope with your problems. Also, regardless of how far you feel you have fallen from grace, you can come back up. Only, I must warn you, you will come back to a much higher level of belief and a much deeper sense of faith and commitment. You will never be the same as you were before. You will also find you have strength which you never believed possible and a sense of happiness and serenity that will lift you to the highest mountain.

The God-relationship is a constant, intertwining theme throughout each stage of acceptance, and regardless of the degree of faith or the particular creed which guides belief, we who are parents of handicapped children follow a similar pattern of reaction.

Now, let us examine some of the typical stumbling blocks which parents whose children are handicapped trip over.

When Faith in God Is Shaken

Naturally your faith in God is affected by the fact that your child is handicapped! A tragic catastrophe such as this tends to weaken the very foundations of your faith. Frequently, it is those who have a strong belief in God who fall into the deepest pit of despair, for their faith is shaken the most. Because their faith has been so important and so real to them, now they wonder, "Is this how my faith and obedience are to be repaid?" It is very typical for parents to consider this as having happened to them personally, not as something that has happened to their child. Therefore, they believe, it is what God has allowed to be done to them.

In the beginning the prayers are to make the child well, to guide the doctors into finding the cure — and faith is strong that God will answer these prayers. Later, when the tests and time prove the child is not cured, and he suffers from a deficiency that will prevent his leading a normal life, there is the feeling of having been deserted by God because the prayers were not answered. "Why? If God is truly a loving God, why would He allow an innocent child to suffer?" Finding no answers, it is simple then to turn away from God, believing that He is not.

As grief lessens and the shock begins to subside, the questioning often follows the line of, "Why is God punishing me?" And because parents feel a personal responsibility for this having happened, in their prayers they ask God to forgive them for their sins. And still the child remains as he was. "Where is God? Is everything I've learned about Him wrong?" Or, "If there really is a God, I cannot trust in Him."

And as guilt turns into hostility, the existence of a Supreme Being cannot actually be denied, but the doubt that He is truly interested in the individual man seems then to become a reality. For those who have felt secure in their faith, the first rumblings of anger toward Him are felt in this mixed-emotion stage, for His rules have been faithfully followed and belief has been strong and true. Then the guilt-imps rise up again to assault with the thoughts of "Man is not supposed to feel this way" and "It is wrong to doubt." But still there are no answers, and solace is not to be found. In despair, perhaps, you turned away from God, placing your trust in yourself and in other men. "God has forsaken me, therefore I cannot believe in Him. I can no longer put my trust in Him to guide me."

If you, as have so many others of us, followed this general pattern, you may then feel so ashamed of your feelings and doubts that you hesitate even to turn to those who are most qualified to help you find the answers. How can you bring yourself to confess to a clergyman that you not only do not believe in God and His mercy, but that a part of you actually hates Him for what He has allowed to happen to you? And, you cease then to bother any more to pray, and turn your back to Him.

By rejecting God you are truly alone, and you are afraid now in your depth of despair at the bottom of a black pit of aloneness and hopelessness. There is nothing left with which to fight, nothing for you to hold on to, and the burdens are becoming overpowering.

Now — you are ready to listen. You are ready to tune in on God's wavelength. Let me assure you again that He is still here: He has been all along. He has not forgotten you, and in His infinite wisdom He understands; with His all-compassing love, He forgives you. But — you must be ready to ask Him for His help and to listen to Him. Listen not only for the response that you want from Him, but for that which He tells you. "Not my will, but Thine, oh Lord."

Stop asking, "Why?" Accept the fact that this has happened and go on from here. Nothing chases faith away as surely as the question "Why?" Open your heart and listen. From this depth of despair and aloneness often comes the bright light of hope and faith which has been strengthened by renewal. You have to work at the task — renewing faith is a task, and no one but you can do it. Don't beat yourself with remorse because of your lack of faith — pray that He will help you have more faith. And don't make up your mind about what the answer to your prayers will be. His answer will come, and to each of us who asks, the answers come in different ways — yours will be in a way that is uniquely yours.

Now, let's go back a few ideas and examine those feelings that may be causing you anguish. Consider doubt. To doubt the existence of God is not evil — not even bad, for doubt is the very starting point of renewed and strengthened faith. You cannot doubt that which does not exist, can you? To doubt is actually to think in a positive direction. Going even deeper into thought, when we doubt God's being, we actually are doubting ourselves; doubting our ability to believe in His being strong enough to put our trust in Him. Or, that we are worthy of His love and trust in us.

Now, think through this idea: has God allowed this to happen to you, or to your child? It is your child who is handicapped, not you. Your dreams and aspirations for your child have been broken, but what of those of your child himself, particularly if he is older when this happens to him? You must remember that he is a person in his own right; you cannot live his life for him. You have the responsibility of teaching him, of providing care for his needs, and of loving him — but his soul is not yours. It is true that God has allowed especially heavy responsibilities to be placed upon your shoulders because of what has happened to your child. But as an adult, you are also expected to have the wisdom to ask Him for help and guidance in carrying out these responsibilities — He does not expect you to bear this burden alone.

Believe me, I have been right there at the bottom of the pit of despair and know from experience how one can lose faith and then find unbelievable strength through renewed faith. (Although, to "misplace" one's faith is actually more accurate than to "lose" it.)

Our Kathy was about eight years old, and she was finally walking and feeding herself, although her speech was still rather unintelligible, and her toilet-training had not progressed much beyond the toddler stage. We did not know yet what her mental ability was, but I suspected it was low. I felt I'd accepted my daughter's handicap quite well and was rather proud of my "adjustment." Finally, however, I began to realize that I was deluding myself, for I was becoming emotionally and physically exhausted and quite depressed. Kathy had then been home about nine months after having spent a year in a boarding school which offered an intensive, one-year training program for cerebral palsied children. Since returning, she had been enrolled in a special class in the public school system — but only for half days because of her "bathroom problem." Few days passed that I'd not be phoned to come to school and bring her home because she'd had an accident. Our life really was in a mess — she wasn't benefiting much from her school experience, I was driving twenty-five miles three times a week to take her to therapy, our oldest son was in first grade and not making a good adjustment to school at all. I was tired and frustrated and my "crabbiness" wasn't helping the deteriorating communication between my husband and me. The only one of the family who was not being adversely affected by the circumstances was our second son — a happy, healthy one-year old. We knew our present plans for Kathy were not good, but neither my husband nor I knew what to do to correct the situation. In my inward-looking frame of mind, I could talk to no one, not even to my husband. I was alone as far as human help was concerned, and I'd ceased to ask God for help because I'd lost my faith in Him.

Then, one sun-brightened morning in early spring as I was outside hanging up the laundry, God spoke to me. I wasn't even thinking about my problems at the time, I was simply concerned with the task at hand. My chore finished, I stopped to listen to two blue jays in a nearby tree as they joyfully tossed their mating calls back and forth to each other. Gradually, I became aware of all the evidence around me of nature's beginning anew the cycle of life. The sweet peas had burst into bloom overnight, covering the back fence with a blanket of fresh color and filling the yard with their gentle fragrance. The swollen buds of the peach tree were showing the pink promise of fruit to come. I looked up to admire the intense blueness of the freshly washed sky and heard my thoughts saying, "All right, Lord, you sent me this child, now tell me what to do with her. You take over, I can't handle it anymore." I was frightened — how dare I talk to Him in that manner, even in the secrecy of my thoughts? Still, I reasoned, He'd already heard me and that was just exactly the way I felt. I *had* done all I knew to do, and now I was at the end of my rope. Since He had allowed me to get into this mess, He could just take over and guide my actions. And He did just that.

It was a strange feeling, like none I'd ever experienced before. Almost immediately I felt a lightening of spirit, as if a tremendous burden had been lifted. I knew with a deep surety that from then on, the situation would work out. I felt sure of myself again, but it was with a different, more certain confidence — I knew I was no longer alone. Now, I still did not know what I was going to do, what action I would take toward correcting the situation, but I knew I would know what to do when the right time came, and I was content then to relax and wait. That night my husband asked me, "What happened today? You seem happier than I've seen you in ages." I told him about my morning's experience. It was hard for him to understand — impossible, really, because until one has a similar experience, he cannot know that he can truly put his hand in the hand of the Lord.

From that day on our lives began to change as odd pieces of the jigsaw puzzle fell into proper place. Often, without obvious rhyme or reason, solutions became apparent. Never again have I felt alone and lost.

I realize there are some readers who question the way I felt, and some who will feel I was being blasphemous in what I said and how I spoke to the Lord, but perhaps He was just waiting for me to reach the point where I was at the end of my own resources so I could relax and let Him direct my thoughts, let Him take over. Looking back, I realize I had to reach that depth of despair from which I knew no way out and could no longer rely upon my own resources, before I could ask and then be ready to listen to His answers.

Perhaps the secret, if there is one, is that many of us must find ourselves in a state of complete hopelessness before our senses and minds are cleared, and we can listen when God speaks to us. I am certainly no theologian, and my faith is only the average, run-of-the-mill variety, but I have learned that problems can become mountains, and that perhaps this is what is meant by "faith which will move mountains." Now, I am learning that with God's help, my problem-mountains can be brought down to a manageable size. So, even though you may feel now that your faith in the goodness of the Lord is lost, even though your belief in His existence is weakened, you are not lost to Him, for He still cares what happens to you, and He does indeed answer our pleas for help. Paraphrasing the words of the psalmist, "The Lord is your shepherd, you shall not need to want . . . though you walk through the valley of despair, you need feel afraid no more, for He is there to comfort you and to lead you onto the safe path" — if you will only let Him. You have only to ask Him for the help you need, and then you must be willing to listen so you can hear His answer. That is all: simple, yet as complex as the world is old. I can assure you, however, that when you do learn to ask for God's help, and then to trust Him to guide you, you will discover you have inner strength which you never even dreamed possible — you will move those mountains.

Tuning in on God's Wavelength

Now, suppose that you are among the fortunate ones who do not lose your faith in God, or have your belief weakened; or else, through your struggle toward acceptance you've found your belief and faith have been restored — you still cannot relax, because the battle is not yet won. You must still strive to keep that delicate balance between man-directed action and God-directed thought, and there are still pitfalls to be avoided.

One of the deeper pitfalls is the "Chosen People" concept — the belief that "God chose me to be this handicapped child's parent." Now, it may well be true that the Lord did choose you to be this particular child's parent — many of us who are parents of handicapped children do feel this way. We often find great solace in our belief that we were especially selected for this role, perhaps because we can then also believe that God would not have chosen us unless He knew we were capable. This belief helps strengthen our faith in Him and our trust that we only have to ask and we shall receive His help and guidance.

The danger in this pitfall is the belief that "since God sent this handicapped child to me, He therefore expects me to be responsible for his cure." Or, "If only I have enough faith, God will cure my child." Following this line of thought, the parents may then refuse the necessary help from the doctors, therapists, and teachers, praying instead for a miraculous cure overnight. When parents follow this line of thought — believing prayer and faith alone are enough to cure their child — they close the doors to other avenues of help which also might be inspired by God. And, they also place themselves in the position of being open to guilt-imps — that their faith is not strong enough, that something must be lacking within themselves because God does not answer their prayers. Let me pose a question: in this "do nothing" attitude, could it not be that parents who feel this way are closing their ears to the guidance God is giving to them? Would it not be better to utilize the skills and knowledge of those people trained in the art of helping children who are handicapped, while also continuing to pray for guidance from God?

Another danger in following the "Chosen People" attitude is that by concentrating all one's time and energies on the care of this one child, there is then no time left for functioning in the other roles which the parents must fill. This is more often the situation with mothers than with fathers, because it is the mother's job to care for the child. Would God really want a mother to ignore the needs of her other children? Are they not also important, even though they have no handicap? Or, what about her role as her husband's wife? And there are the other roles which must also be recognized such as a participating member of the church, a concerned citizen in the community, a friend to others in need, and so on? Are these not also God-chosen roles?

These questions lead right into a question which often is predominant in a parent's mind — "Why?" Not, "Why did God punish me by letting my child be handicapped," but "Why was *I* chosen? What was the Lord's purpose? What does He expect me to do because of what I have learned as a result of this experience?" In other words, "What is God's will for me?" This is fine, it is good positive thinking — so long as the heart and mind is kept open to hear God. Too often the search for finding the purpose becomes a justification for a sense of personal failure, rather than a willingness to carry out God's will. Then the deeds are man-directed, rather than God-inspired.

Don't sit back and expect God to do it all. Rather than praying for a miracle that will make your child whole, pray for guidance in choosing the best doctors, the clinic or school which is best suited to your child's particular needs. Ask Him to show you the way to make the best decisions. Ask, too, for strength to meet and overcome the problems. Pray that you have the emotional strength and physical energy you need to carry out the therapy and training on the home program. Ask for guidance in adjusting your life pattern to fit the situation. Sometimes we need very practical guidance, such as help in finding a way to meet the financial obligations. Everyone needs His help in overcoming moods of depression and despair so that the future can be anticipated with confidence of security and happiness. Pray, too, then for hope.

Don't worry that your faith might not be strong enough, for praying and meditation will strengthen it. (And who of us can know how much faith is enough?) Don't fret because you feel you do not have the depth of faith that moves mountains, maybe you do not know what the mountains are — perhaps you are moving mountains and thinking they are only mole-hills. Have faith that God is, and that He is concerned about you. Trust in Him to answer your prayers for help — even those times when you ask Him to help you have faith!

Having a child who is handicapped is a tragic circumstance, regardless of the cause or the type of the deficiency. Seldom is a person's faith in God put to such a stern test; and yet, being forced by this circumstance to look beyond the limited range of shallow thinking for new understanding, one is then able to find a greater depth of faith. Because of this deeper faith, one can then be guided by the Lord into a fuller realization of his talents, and a widening and strengthening of character. One can then tune in on the Lord's wavelength.

"Why did God let this happen?" It happened; the past is over, it is done and cannot be undone. Your concern is not *why* He allowed this to happen, your concern should be with what you are going to do now that it has happened. Are you going to give in to defeat, or are you going to return God's love of you by letting Him help you to develop something good and worthwhile out of this tragedy?

"Why is God punishing me?" You may be punishing your-self in His name.

"Why does He let an innocent child suffer?" The parents suffer more than does the child. It is the responsibility of parents to see that their child does not suffer — love your child, and let him know that you do.

"Is there a God?" There surely is. Do not be afraid of your doubt, for it is only human to doubt. The Lord knows this, for He understands the weaknesses of men, and He has proven over and over that He forgives those who doubt Him. Remember — to doubt is to open the doors of the mind to believe.

"But is He really concerned with me and my problems?" Of course He is! If He cares about the birds in the field, He surely cares about you. Talk to Him, tune in on His wavelength and listen to Him — you'll know.

Your Relationship with Other Believers

So far we have been discussing the personal relationship to the Lord, but what about one's relationships with other people who also are believers?

Your husband, or your wife, for example. It is very easy to overlook the fact that no two people have the same degree of faith at the same time. A wife may have found a deeper level of her faith, as I did, but because her husband has not had a similar experience, he is still groping along on another level. How tempting it is to try to force one's own beliefs on another — especially when that person is also deeply loved. And, how easy it is to lose patience when the other one seems to not be trying to enlarge his faith.

Mary and John were in this sort of trap. They were both raised in religion-oriented families and carried their childhood beliefs and practices into adulthood. During the early years of their marriage, they were very active communicants and contributed much to their parish. After their first child was born with physical and mental handicaps, they found great solace through their church and their faith. Then John was transferred to another city. Settling into a new environment and job, becoming acquainted with a new circle of friends, and all the adjustments one makes when moving, consumed their time; and church attendance was postponed from one week to the next, until nearly a year passed and they had not found a church. In the meantime, their daughter Beth was growing and her handicap was becoming more noticeable, her need for treatment and therapy more pressing, her behavior harder to control. The stress and strain finally became too much for Mary, and she broke emotionally. After months of counseling, and Beth's being placed in a residential school where she received the necessary training and therapy, Mary became strong enough to manage. During this time of such anguish, they had found a church and had begun to attend regularly. Mary found her faith restored and strengthened, but John's grew weaker until he could no longer attend services, and any discussion about religion angered him. Mary worried about John, of course, for she loved him and wanted him to find the peace and strength which she was finding through her renewed faith. The more he rejected religion, the more she worried about her own inadequacy to meet her responsibility to help him. They were growing farther and farther apart as man and wife, he was spending more and more time at his job, their social life became nonexistent, and John was spending less time at home even though they now had a new son. Mary finally had a long talk with her minister.

"You are pushing John too much, Mary," he told her. "He has not had the opportunity to develop his faith, as you did, and he feels inadequate. By trying to make him believe as strongly as you do, you are forcing him to build up stronger and stronger defenses. Ease up on him. Stop preaching, and start showing him by example. Put into practice all you have learned about treating others with love. Pray for John, of course, but don't push him. Give him the respect he deserves as a person, and show him the love you feel for him as your husband. Be patient and be concerned about your own relationship with God."

Mary was wise enough to take her pastor's advice, and relieved of the pressure of guilt which Mary had been forcing on him, John was able to work out his problems concerning religion. He may never reach the depth of faith Mary has found, but he is now able to work toward that end.

"I'm never going to church again! I've had enough of the way those hypocrites there treat my child — the remarks they make, the way they stare. It's as if they think she doesn't belong there with them." Why do we expect people, just because they are sitting in church, to be any more able to express themselves in a manner that makes us feel more comfortable? It is the rare person, and usually someone who has had firsthand experience, who does not feel ill-at-ease in the presence of a person who is handicapped. Why? The answer often is simply that they don't know what to say and are afraid of saying the wrong things. In an attempt to be kind, many are oversolicitous, while others may turn away and so appear to be cruel. This is a very delicate area of communication, for feelings are so very exposed and sensitive. The responsibility of setting the tone of reaction lies with you, the parent, just as in social situations. By your attitude you determine the kind of response others give to your child. Remember the discussion about shame? How a matter-of-fact, accepting attitude on the part of the parents relieves the embarrassment others often feel? So it is in church-related situations. If you walk into church or temple with your handicapped child, feeling that perhaps he really doesn't belong there, or embarrassed by him and by what you fear others will say, you will surely find opposition. Usually, the opposition or rejection of others is an imagined reaction, but a defiant or defensive attitude on your part tends to elicit an adverse reaction from others. Your response to other people is guided by those unseen and unheard lines of communication which we all emit. Be sure that yours are not negative, for it is not always other people's problem when your child seems to be rejected — it is more often yours.

Regardless of what you may say or of what your own attitude may be, there will be some who do not accept your child — because they cannot. Here again you help more by your example than by your words. The person who turns away from your child, or says something cruel and unkind, may have his own personal roadblocks — fear that this may happen to a child of his, guilt because he is glad he is not in your shoes. In such instances you can do little except to pay him the respect of letting him work out his own problems.

Above all else, do put your own surface feelings aside and think of your child. You know, it is not absolutely necessary that your handicapped child attend church with you all the time. Sometimes we take our children to services more for ourselves than for our child. Kathy made me aware of this. We always have her home for Christmas, and it was important to me that we all attend the family Christmas Eve service together. It is a long service and always crowded. Kathy would fidget, then become increasingly irritable and noisy, and the boys would be embarrassed by their sister's attention-attracting behavior. Each year attending this service grew to be more and more of an unpleasant chore, rather than being a joy. The last year that we followed this family tradition, the service was about half over when Kathy turned to me and said (loudly, because she cannot whisper) "Please, go home? I don't like it here." I realized then that we were there, not for her sake, not for family unity, but because I liked the feeling of sitting there surrounded by my entire family. (And, to be perfectly honest, deep down I was proud of the impression I knew I was giving to others by proving I was not ashamed of my handicapped child.) To satisfy our own egos, my husband and I were putting our children through an agonizing experience. Kathy was not accustomed to sitting still for such a long period, she really was not capable of understanding what was going on, and she was frustrated and confused by so many people, because her life is quiet and among people she knows well. Now, we attend the Christmas morning service — a beautiful ritual, simple and peaceful, and uncrowded. We all look forward to this, and Kathy is usually the first to remind us, "It's time to get ready for church."

Of course, your child should know the Lord, for he is just as much a child of God as are your nonhandicapped children. (Sometimes, I think more so.) Teach him at home as best you can. Read Bible stories to him, sing to him, talk to him about God's love for him. If he can manage to attend the services, fine — don't deny him the opportunity because of your own reluctance, but don't make him endure a situation that is painful to him.

If there is no niche in your church or temple into which your child can comfortably fit, consider the possibility of creating one. Perhaps a chapel service for children only, or a Sunday school class for handicapped children. Teenagers can be marvelous and effective teachers, given a little guidance and training. At this age young people want to help others, and being not too far from childhood themselves, they are able to relate in ways adults cannot. Also, they are not bound by so many inhibitions and can express their gentleness and love. Don't sit back and expect your church to do it all for you. Very few parishes have the personnel or facilities needed for working with handicapped children. Perhaps yours needs your interest and action.

Summary

No one can tell you just how you should feel toward God, for that is a personal relationship. But you can be guided and advised as to what action you can take which may help in your understanding, and you will certainly profit through help in interpreting and understanding the Bible and your church teachings. Through prayers composed by others, you can find expression of your own needs when your thoughts have eluded you. But determining the quality of your relationship with God is your responsibility. You must learn how to open the door to your heart so He can come in. You must learn to listen. The words of the greatest prayer, or one that is simply appropriate to your needs, will have no meaning for you if you will not listen.

Forgive yourself for your doubts. Realize that only through the questioning aroused by doubt can you attain a better understanding of God. Doubting is positive — one cannot doubt that which he does not believe exists.

Forgive yourself, too, for your blame and your resentment toward God. He forgives you, and in doubting this, you are only doubting yourself and your worth as a person.

Accept the truth that your prayers are answered. His answer may not be what you have asked for, but He does answer in the manner which is best for you. (That's a hard concept to accept, isn't it?) Only through faith can one believe this.

You may have forsaken God, but He has not forsaken you — He is still here, but you have to ask Him for His help and guidance. Only when you are ready to ask, are you ready to listen.

Concerning the close and intimate relationship between husband and wife, do not expect the other one to have the same degree of faith at the same time as you have. If one of you is having trouble reconciling human feelings and reactions to his concept of God, be understanding of the travail and be patient. His soul and his God-relationship is his responsibility, just as yours is yours alone. Reveal through your actions, not just in attempted verbal communication, the security and love and trustful peace you feel.

Be patient, too, with other people who act in ways you feel they should not toward your child and you. Understand that other people all too often react negatively because they do not know how to express themselves positively. Feel sympathy toward them, not antagonism. Show them by your own manner how to accept your child.

Continue to pray — even when you doubt that your prayers

are being answered, or that they are even being heard. Perhaps it is not that God doesn't hear your pleas, but rather that you aren't listening. Relax, don't block the gateway to your heart by your own worries and resentment. And, in your prayers, look for something to thank Him for — despite how you may feel, you do have many blessings and much to be thankful for.

Listen to your heart, for it is through your conscience that He speaks. "But how will I know when God is speaking to me?" If you can strip away your self-directed thoughts and think only about God, you can hear Him so clearly you will know. Once having prepared yourself, many times the first thought you have is God's. You may never know with a sure certainty that it is God who is directing your thoughts, but this is where faith enters. A very wise priest once gave me this hint which I will pass on to you — when meditating, select one verse from the Bible which has meaning for you. Repeat this verse over and over until you have cleared your mind of other thoughts. For me, the verse I use most often is the beginning of Psalm 23, "The Lord is my shepherd, I shall not want." For me this means the Lord is here, I do not have to go out and find Him.

3. Especially for Wives

PARENTHOOD, EVEN WHEN there are no unusual problems with a child, places strain and stresses upon the relationship between husband and wife. But there is the other side, too — parenthood also can increase and intensify the depth of love, concern, and respect that parents feel toward each other and add meaning and purpose to the life they are building together.

When a child is handicapped, it is only natural that exceptional strain will be placed on the parents' relationship with each other. There are many reasons for this, but generally it is because neither is prepared for this abrupt, often catastrophic, change in the life they had expected, and also, because of the very intensity of emotion, the threats to self-esteem and security, each parent is forced to come to grips with every facet of his personality — the weak as well as the strong.

Some marriages, already weakened by other types of forces, need only the catalyst of a handicapped child for destruction. Other marriages not only survive, but become stronger and richer because the handicapping condition of their child provides a different sort of catalytic influence, one which pulls the parents together as they respond to each other's needs.

Being very realistic — because your child is handicapped, your need for reliance upon your husband is greater, just as your child's need for a warmly harmonious home life is greater. Few other circumstances in a woman's life make it so vitally important that the relationship between husband and wife be healthy and loving, and few other circumstances hold so many inherent reasons for conflict.

Because you are a wife and mother, the responsibility for creating a happy home atmosphere rests predominantly on you, for you set the tone of the atmosphere in your home and in your marriage. Where do you begin, and what can you do to insure that the home life you create will be loving and harmonious?

You begin with yourself and your own inner feelings — this is what was discussed in Part I and what you strive to accomplish all along your road to acceptance. To be successful, you must resolve to learn to be strong enough to direct your major concern toward others rather than toward yourself and particularly toward your husband.

You begin also with the relationship that bonds you and your husband into the unit that is at the head of the family. Yours is not the sole responsibility, of course, your husband must also contribute his efforts, but you can have the greater influence, and by your own words and actions, you will do much to determine the quality of your marriage.

Understanding Your Husband's Reactions

To gain an insight into how you can be a true helpmate to your husband, you must first have some understanding of how he feels and what his reactions are to having a child who is handicapped.

You are not the only parent — your husband is the father of this child, and he has his own fears and apprehensions about being a parent of a child who is handicapped. He, too, meets roadblocks and falls over stumbling blocks along his road to acceptance, just as you do, and while many of his feelings are similar to yours, many are different and uniquely his.

He feels guilty for many of the same reasons you do, but some of his guilt-imps assume a different character from yours. He also blames himself for this having happened and may be tormented by thoughts of what he did to cause his child's handicap and what he possibly could have done to prevent it. At times he also blames you and then feels guilty because he holds you responsible, knowing it is wrong to do so.

Your husband, too, feels resentment that this should happen and deny him the full joy of having a "normal" son or daughter. (And the father's resentment and anguish is usually greater if the child is a son.) He, too, must learn how to conceal that sadness he experiences when he looks at his child and is reminded again that his hopes and dreams for his child's future have been destroyed. (And remember, a man is not supposed to cry — he is expected to be strong.) He, just as you, must learn to redirect his goals of ambition for this child, and often this is a much harder task for a father than for a mother.

This has been quite a blow to his sense of self-worth and has affected, to a greater or lesser degree, his confidence in himself and in his ability to function as a man.

Just as you have your fears, so does your husband have his. He may be afraid, especially at the beginning, that he will not be strong enough to handle whatever the future may have in store for him as a father. (And, although most men find this hard to admit, one of the most frequent fears is of losing their wives' love and being replaced by the child in her concern.)

One of a father's major fears is financial responsibility. It is a rare family that can easily absorb the enormous extra expenses incurred when a child is handicapped. Most parents must struggle to work these expenses into the budget, and perhaps learn to swallow pride and accept (or even seek) financial help. Your husband knows he must in some way meet the burden of these added financial obligations, and the effects of this responsibility touch him in ways you may not consider. For example, because his job security must now be assured, he may have lost his freedom of choice of career or occupation and must follow the safe and sure route of remaining in a closed-in job offering only a limited challenge to him and his ability. Or, to meet the financial obligations, he must work harder and longer hours, under the pressure of the necessity of being successful.

You worry about your child's future, of course, but your husband's worries often are deeper and more ominous, for the child's welfare is primarily his responsibility. He knows he may be faced with providing for residential schooling or long years of expensive treatment and training. If there is little or no possibility of your child being independent, he worries about the child's care if something should happen to his earning power or to him. These are a father's responsibilities, and these thoughts are always with him, even if he should — as does happen — give up and try to run away from his obligations to his family. Is it any wonder then, that he becomes depressed and morose when he thinks of the unrelieved financial burdens stretching out until the end of his days?

So you see, in many ways your husband has his own particular set of fears and worries. These worries often lie behind his moods of withdrawal from you, and also do much to explain why he struggles so hard against accepting the fact of his child's handicap.

Helping Your Husband along the Road to Acceptance

Now, what are some of the ways in which you may be able to help your husband as he struggles to accept the fact of his child's handicap?

In the beginning as you comfort and console him in his grief, assure him of the rightness of his feelings, and let him cry with you. Regardless of how many sympathetic and understanding friends and relatives are there for you to lean on, turn to your husband first for comfort and consolation in your grief. Let him know you are depending upon him and his strength to help you. Go back and read the chapter "Grief," replacing yourself and your feelings with your husband and his. Be patient with your husband while you are striving to help him understand that his child is different, and don't neglect helping him find encouragement and hope of the future.

Help Him Learn the Facts   Some women, believing that they should protect their husbands, attempt to shield them from the truth. This is unfair to the father because in the first place, he has a right to know — this is his child, too. In the second place, this approach only makes it harder for him to accept the reality later, for hard fact is easier to digest when administered in small doses. Just as the quality of your acceptance greatly depends upon the extent of your understanding, and your understanding is contingent upon your knowledge of the facts, so does your husband's. This may not be a problem in your particular situation, but it has been my experience that few men have the time or the inclination to act as fact-finders themselves. Even physician-fathers often rely upon their wives to gather information when their own children are involved.

Encourage your husband to go with you to consultations and conferences with the doctors so he will have the opportunity to hear the facts straight from the source. It is vitally necessary for his own acceptance and consequent adjustment that he talk to the doctors at some point, so use your womanly wiles if you must to get him there. He no doubt will have his own questions to be answered which you would not think of asking for him. Don't expect him to go with you to every appointment unless he really wants to — often the first and the final consultation with a particular specialist is sufficient.

If your husband balks and refuses to go, discuss this with the doctors (or your counselor) and enlist their aid. They will have met this reaction before — it is not at all unusual father behavior — so listen to what they advise.

Later, if your child is in a therapy program, encourage your husband to talk with the therapist from time to time, so he will have a better understanding of the purpose and the projected aims as well as of the progress his child is making. He may benefit by attending one of the therapy sessions, for not only will this help him to accept the reality of his child's handicap, but also he will be reassured of the value of the therapy and encouraged because he will know something is being done to help his child. Similarly, when other types of treatment are prescribed, his understanding of the purpose, the expected progressive development, and the need of the treatment will help him reach a clearer understanding of the whole picture. And don't forget — you need his counsel to help make decisions. Don't deny him this right of parenthood.

Sharing Your Child with Your Husband You share your heartache, your fears, and your disappointment with your husband, also share your child with him. Spending time with your child, watching him grow and develop, working with him has helped you in your acceptance and adjustment, has it not? So will having the opportunity to become acquainted with his child help your husband in his acceptance and adjustment. Being able to express your love to your child by caring for his needs, playing with him, comforting and loving him has eased some of your hurt, and so will your husband's hurt be eased by showing love to his son or daughter.

Child care, especially during the early years, is a mother's responsibility, but it is a father's privilege. Feeding, dressing, bathing your child will help your husband get to know him and feel more comfortable with him, so let him take over these chores sometimes. When there are home exercises to be done, as in the instance of an orthopedically handicapped child, save one session to be done in the evening after your husband returns from work or in the morning before he leaves. Hold to the schedule whenever possible — that particular time is his to spend with his child.

But the time your husband spends with your child should not be all work: both need time for play, too, for playing with his child also helps establish that all-important line of communication. Be sure you give your husband an opportunity to share in the fun and pleasures of parenthood.

What you actually do makes little difference — sharing the child is the important goal to be reached. Your handicapped child needs to be cared for by both parents and to know the love of each. And, there is another important reason for sharing — both of you will feel more secure if you know that should something happen to incapacitate you, he would be experienced enough to cope with the situation alone.

Some men may not want to share child care, preferring to leave these tasks in their wives' hands. If your husband seems to prefer to watch from a distance, take it easy with him. Don't push — try to discover why he feels as he does so you will be guided in your efforts to encourage him. He may just need more time to sort out his own thinking.

Making an effort to present your child as favorably as possible to your husband may help. Rather than bathing him in the morning when it suits your own schedule, you might bathe him later in the day so he is fresh and clean when your husband comes home. Or, if your child's "fussy time" is late in the day, as with most children, give him a tide-over snack in the afternoon. These are only suggestions — just remember that your objective is to find ways to help your husband adjust to having a child who is handicapped.

Discipline Should also Be Shared Discipline is a two-parent responsibility, and a child's sense of security is strengthened when he knows that his father, as well as his mother, cares enough about him to set and maintain acceptable limits of behavior. And both parents will feel more at ease with their handicapped child if they know they are free to accept the responsibility of teaching these limits, even when punishment is necessary.

Some fathers need to be prodded into assuming their responsibility for discipline, others need to be quietly restrained from setting unrealistic limits of behavior or from meting out punishment that is too harsh. Neither the limits of acceptable behavior, nor the punishment can always be predetermined, of course, but it is important that the parents agree as to the general limits and the general approach to discipline when the child exceeds these limits. Discipline is one of those important issues which should be discussed by both parents with the child's teachers and therapists, and with the doctors and psychologists, for until they have some understanding of the extent of control and understanding their child is capable of learning, they cannot know what limits can be reasonably set.

*

Your responsibility to your child is great, but so is your responsibility to your husband. His concern must be divided between his job and his family, leaving less time for him to think and work out the problems of his adjustment to having a handicapped child. Because you are with your child more, your attention is more concentrated on the whole scope of his handicapping condition, giving you more opportunity to develop insight into the problems of adjustment. Thinking of your husband with love and compassion and putting his need for understanding ahead of your own response to his reactions, you will then be free to discover ways of helping him.

The Wife-to-Husband Relationship

Most of the above has been concerned with how you can help your husband with his adjustment to having a handicapped child, but what about the relationship between the two of you? Involved as you are with the care for your child and the worry about his development, it is easy to let your role of wife slide. The need to be a mother is obvious and demanding, the need to be a wife is more subtle and less demanding. Yet, the obligations of being a wife are equally important.

The strain placed upon your marriage by the unusual problems of your child's handicap will be lasting and severe. Counterbalancing the inevitable stressful effect this will have on the relationship between you and your husband gives you an exceptional opportunity to develop your role of wife to the highest level of quality. Every facet of wifehood becomes important now — homemaker, companion, helpmate, mistress. Your success will depend upon the amount of effort and thought you expend, and the extent of your willingness to concentrate on meeting your husband's need of you.

It is by paying attention to the smaller aspects of your role that you will achieve success in building a strong marriage, for these are the ways by which you let your husband know he is important to you. The way you welcome him when he comes home at night may seem to be insignificant, but your manner tells him whether he is important to you or not and determines the tone of the relationship between you. Laying aside the project you are working on so you can listen to what he is saying may not seem to be very important, but if he must make an effort to gain your attention, he may feel, "Why bother?" Your at-home grooming, your housekeeping skills, the meals you prepare are all important and should not be taken lightly.

Even more so than if your child were not handicapped, both of you need the security of a good marital relationship, assured of understanding, love, and concern for each other — a relationship in which the strength of one reinforces the other.

You, because you are a woman, have sources of strength that are denied your husband, and he has his own strength to contribute. As you strive to develop your strength in ability to give love and understanding to your husband, so will the quality of his love for and understanding of you grow in strength.

When Marriage Fails

There are times when nothing that a wife can do will preserve her marriage. Although love and concern are necessary, marriage is a partnership and, as with any other type of partnership, to be successful both participants must contribute their efforts. Love, respect, understanding, and concern cannot be one-sided if the relationship is to be meaningful, satisfying, and enduring. There are men who cannot accept their role as the father of a handicapped child, regardless of any effort their wives may expend toward helping them. And, there are instances in which the basic personalities of husband and wife could never be made to blend together, even in the best of circumstances.

If you should feel that your marriage is beginning to deteriorate, don't wait until the problems have grown too great for any hope of solution; seek the counsel of someone trained and experienced in helping heal ailing marriages.

There are marriages where the unhealthiness is beyond even the most adept professional help, and the only solution is separation or divorce. But, remember this — just as the advent of a child cannot make a weak marriage strong, neither can a child, even one who is handicapped, destroy a strong marriage. When a marriage fails, it is not because the child is handicapped — the cause is much more complex than that and lies within the parents themselves.

4. Especially for Mothers

BEING A MOTHER is a demanding job, full of great responsibility and much self-denial — but the rewards far outweigh the drawbacks. This will be true for you, too, if you will train yourself to look for the sunshine rather than seeing only the darker side of your life. Your child, handicapped though he is, will open the door for you to a life that can be rich in happiness and love. Sure, there will be plenty of times when you will have to consciously look for benefits and rewards, and you must learn not to use the usually accepted criteria of measuring the achievements of motherhood as your guidelines, for your situation is unique, and you are as special as is your child.

This role will demand much of you in many instances. There will be times when you will feel you cannot go on any longer because the burden of your responsibilities seems heavier than you are capable of carrying. You will become depressed at times when your child seems to be making no progress, when you can see no possibility for the future to be different from the present.

Let me assure you of this, however — these moments will grow less frequent and of less intensity as time passes and as you learn how to meet your problems. You *shall* find the strength of will and of character. You are much more capable than you think. Have confidence in yourself as Mother.

Don't look toward the future and wonder how you will be able to manage: learn to recognize and appreciate each day's small gains and to be content to wait to set tomorrow's goals. Then you will find the peace that will enable you to see the joys in your life.

Happiness is a goal everyone strives to reach, and it will not be denied to you; rather, you will know that exquisite state of mind with an intensity denied to most. You will learn, too, that happiness is not what others give to you, but what you give to others. And, yes, the time will come when you can count your blessings.

Many of your blessings will not be tangible and easily discernible, but they will give you riches far greater than mere wealth, for these will be ways in which you will grow and mature in your manner of approaching life, and because they are refinements of your character, they cannot be taken from you.

You will learn patience, and in so doing you will become more tolerant of yourself and of others. You will know the self-satisfaction of accomplishing achievements that you once thought were far beyond your capability. Because you have lived through so many times of utter hopelessness, you will have invincible hope for and faith in the future.

And perhaps the greatest blessing of all — you will learn the meaning of that elusive and indefinable emotion, love, in the full sense of the meaning. And, as you become more sure of yourself, you will know the importance of love freely given and shared by you as well as of the love you receive.

All this may sound fanciful and abstract and wishful to you now, but these are only some of the rewards and blessings you will receive as you strive to adjust to being a mother of a child who is handicapped. You have been given a challenge — one you certainly did not ask to have, but which is yours nevertheless. You have only two choices now: either you can give up and succumb to defeat, or you can accept the challenge and go forward to conquer the new goals which lie ahead.

Exercise Your Right to Love Your Child

As a mother you have certain rights, and not the least of these is your right to love your child. Now, doesn't that seem a strange thing to say, because it is so obviously true? But think about it: are you so torn between your desire to do everything right for your child and your fear that you won't that your desire to cuddle and love him is pushed into the background?

Remember the discussion about loving your handicapped child in the chapter entitled "Rejection"? Remember how important it is to the child that he be mothered and physically loved? From this grows his feeling of security of your love of him; from this also grows your love of him and your simple pleasure and enjoyment of your child as he is. So, don't be afraid to take time off to express your love to your child. Hold him, sing to him, talk to him, feel free to relax and give vent to all your tender feelings of motherhood.

Love is so very complex, even when concerning the relationship between mother and child — especially when concerning that relationship. Love is your acceptance of him as he is with all his inabilities as well as his abilities: love is also responding to his love for you.

This child of yours is going to have a hard row ahead of him as he grows up, and he is going to need all the help from other people he can get. By showing him you love him in the way he can understand best — your outward and visible expressions — you will give him the security of knowing he is lovable. Having learned he can respond freely to your expressed love, he will then be able to extend his own love freely to others. With that love, comes trust.

Now, don't overdo your loving of him. Try to keep that balance between too much and not enough and love expressed in the right manner. You don't want to smother your child, and you certainly don't want to overprotect him — excessive coddling retards growth and development just as too little love does. He has so much to learn, and where else to learn except in the safety of the home where he is protected by that blanket of security that is love and acceptance? If he is crippled in his legs, he must learn to try to walk; if he is blind, he must learn how to take care of his own needs; if he is deaf, he must learn how to communicate with others who can hear; if he is mentally retarded, he must learn self-discipline and how to stay within the limits of his independence while learning to develop and use the ability he has. If a child is coddled and protected so that he cannot make the attempt, he will never learn how to pick himself up after falling or even make the attempt.

There is another danger — that of letting your ambition for his development override your desire to love him. Sometimes we fall into the trap of being so concerned with what we are attempting to do *for* our child that we cannot see what we are doing *to* him. Running here to take him to physical therapy training, dashing there to get him to his special class on time, all the exercises to be done at home, and the extra training and teaching of the home program leave little time or energy for showing love. Worrying about whether or not enough time is being spent with the child, or if more time would mean more progress, is an affliction common to all mothers and especially to mothers whose children are handicapped.

Many times it is not so much what is done that is important, but the manner in which it is done. So it is with showing love to your child. A smile, rather than a grim look of determination; a quick rumple of his hair and "That's good, son!" rather than a stern admonition that he is not trying hard enough; a hug and kiss at bedtime or just in passing for no reason at all — how long do these take?

And don't overlook the opportunities to combine love cuddling with need supplying. For example, mealtime is a natural opportunity to show affection. Just the fact that the child is being held in his mother's arms to be fed gives him a sense of security in being loved and cared for. Bathtime is another time when it is natural to show affection. It is pleasurable for the baby or child and can actually be fun for the parents.

Even severely mentally retarded children respond to affection. When we were searching for the right residential school for our

Kathy, the most outstanding feature of the school we finally chose was the atmosphere of love. I've watched with frank amazement at what some of the teachers and therapists there have accomplished with the children, many of whom were considered "hopelessly retarded" by other experts. If strangers who are only substitute parents can do so much through the free and liberal application of loving affection, think how much more parents can accomplish within the home.

Exercise your right to love your child, show him affection, but do not abuse this privilege.

Discipline

Discipline is an important part of love, too. Children who have not been taught the restraint of discipline often are insecure and doubtful of their parents' love of them. Ideally, discipline should be administered within the framework of love and affection; realistically, this is often a most difficult task. Nevertheless, by ignoring discipline you withhold your love from your child just as surely as if you never cuddle him or tell him you love him.

Your child's ability to profit from training and therapy will depend to a great extent upon how well you have taught him the rules of self-discipline. He must learn to be quiet, to listen, to keep the rules of acceptable behavior so he can be taught. He must learn to do the exercises and the therapy even when he would rather not.

Karen was a patient I once worked with as a speech therapist in a clinic. She was about four years old, an adorable, winsome child — so long as everything was going just as she wanted. She became a little brat whenever she was thwarted in doing just exactly as she pleased — and this included even kicking the therapist or pulling her hair! Mentally, she was below average, but well within the educable range, and her speech problems could have been corrected without too much difficulty. But because she had never known the restraints of discipline at home and the limits of her behavior were bounded only by the amount of perseverance and energy she cared to use at that particular time, therapy was impossible for her. Every therapist tried, but to no avail. Group therapy was out of the question, because Karen did not know how to share with anyone else, and her antics so disrupted the sessions that no other child could learn, either. When the clinic director discussed Karen's behavior with her mother, trying to show her the actual harm she was doing to her child by not disciplining her, she withdrew Karen from the clinic. I don't know what happened to either Karen or the family, but I can imagine a life of wasted ability and unhappiness for all, especially for Karen.

Now, as to methods of discipline. There are few hard and fast rules, because each case must stand alone, but there are a few overall guidelines which apply to every child. First, be gentle but firm in your handling of your child. Be as consistent as you can possibly be. Don't set the limits of acceptable behavior too close or too wide. Begin discipline when the child is young, for by the time he is "old enough to understand," he may have grown past the time when the foundation of good self-discipline can be firmly established. (You will, of course, adapt your expectations to his age and level of mental development.)

These are blanket statements, let's look at some a little more closely. How will you know the limits of acceptable behavior which you can reasonably expect? And how can you determine effective methods of teaching your child discipline? You must have some understanding of what ability he has for learning and to what extent his particular handicapping condition will determine his emotional response. So, talk with the doctors, his teachers, the therapists, and counselors. Try to learn as much as you can about the effects of his handicap on his emotional stability. If lack of ability to control muscular activity is part of his particular handicap, you must then accept some degree of hyperactivity and a short attention span. If fear is a major element of his handicap, such as with a blind child, then you will use reassurance as a prime tool in your discipline teaching. Read and study material written about your child's particular handicap and other books about child raising in general and adapt the basic principles to your situation.

Don't try to make your child fit into a preconceived mold of behavior. He is an individual in his own right, and his reaction to stress will be determined by the type of personality he has, by his inabilities caused by his handicap, and by the particular situation causing his stress (and being thwarted is stressful).

Don't let your guilt and self-blame lead you down the erroneous path of believing you owe it to your child to give him everything he wants. You owe your child every reasonable effort you can make to help him be happy, and self-discipline predetermines happiness.

Remember that your child must live in a normal world with normal people. He must learn to adapt as best he can to this world, since it will not adapt to him. That is true in a certain sense whether he continues to live at home or whether a residential school is more appropriate for him. He must learn to control himself because he has so much to learn, and he cannot learn unless he can listen and conform to established standards of behavior.

Now, don't go overboard with your discipline training; watch out for actual cruelty on your part. Oh, yes, that can happen — even to the best of mothers. There will be times when your handicapped child will try your patience more than a non-handicapped child ever could. We want so much for our child who is deficient and are so often frustrated by the fact that we just simply don't know what to do. Also, we are often frustrated because we really do not know how much he is capable of doing or understanding. Nerves are naturally on edge and more sensitive in relation to this particular child. It is hard to control one's temper after having listened to a child cry for two or three hours when everything seems to have been tried to appease whatever is wrong, or when a hyperactive child has driven one almost to the screaming point by his racing through the house and his excessive noisemaking. Rage can overtake even the most well-adjusted mother when her child retaliates by deliberately throwing a favorite vase.

So, while you may have every reason to lose your temper, to be overharsh in your punishment, you must learn to check your actions. There are many ways mothers have learned — or have devised — to give themselves time to gather up their reins of self-control. One very effective method is simply to absent yourself from the child for a few moments. If possible, depending upon the age and condition of the child, walk out of the house for a short breather; look at the sky, observe the cloud formations, admire your rose garden, or just let a cool breeze fan away the heat of anger. Or, if you must stay within sight and hearing of your child, walk into the other room, pick up a book or a magazine, turn on the television, listen to a favorite record — anything that will give you time to catch your breath of reason. Music is also an excellent way to calm the child.

Helping Your Child Develop Self-Esteem

Social Acceptance   Of course, you want your child to be socially acceptable. You don't hide him in an upstairs back room as was done in less enlightened ages. You are not ashamed of having a child who is handicapped, although because he is a reflection on you, you may be ashamed of the impression of himself he presents to the outside world. His social acceptance is important, regardless of the type or the extent of his handicap — for himself, for your adjustment, and for the family's acceptance and adjustment.

Whether handicapped minimally or severely, your child is going to be out in public at some time or another. And, he must learn to be with people other than his immediate family. You cannot always be around to protect him and to run interference for him with people who may not know him well or do not understand his problems. There are his teachers, his therapists, the doctors and nurses, even the baby sitters upon whom he must learn to rely, to respond to, and to communicate with. Also, there are your friends, your husband's friends and associates as well as the friends of his brothers and sisters around whom he must learn how to conduct himself if he is to be a full-fledged member of the family. And especially if he is minimally handicapped, there are the children with whom he plays.

You love this child, and you want other people to at least give him a chance to be accepted, not to reject him just because he is different. That is one reason why you work so hard to teach him good discipline — so he will be well behaved when he is out in public as well as at home and at school. You try to teach him what to do and say, because you know that the sense of security this gives him helps him meet people and handle situations with more confidence. (Knowing that he is loved and accepted by his family also increases his confidence in himself and lets him be more outgoing in his relationship with other people.)

Social acceptance — being liked and responded to with warmth and amicability by people outside his family — is so very important for your child's self-esteem and his evaluation of himself as a person worthy of being liked and accepted for himself despite his handicap. This is infinitely more difficult for the child whose handicap is relatively minor, for he then lives within the fringe of the so-called "normal" world, unlike the severely handicapped child who is able to be only an observer. Even truly mature adults sometimes find it difficult to be tolerant of those less able than they, much less to show real acceptance to someone whose actions they don't understand. Children are more tolerant and accepting of a child who is less able physically than they are than of one who is mentally deficient. They can see and understand the physical handicap, while the mentally handicapped child is mistrusted because of his (to them) unpredictable behavior. I am firmly convinced that a child's rejection of another who is handicapped is not due to an inherent streak of meanness which is said to lie in all of us and which children have not yet learned to control, but is due to his fear of what he does not understand and therefore finds threatening.

If your child is minimally handicapped mentally and therefore able to attend the regular school and to socialize with non-handicapped children, his acceptance by other children is going to be your hardest hurdle to surmount. Unfortunately there is no way you can fully protect him from children who will tease him and taunt him because of his handicap, so somehow you must work to help him develop the inner strength to protect himself. What a simple statement that seems to be, and yet how very complex and how very difficult in actuality. I cannot tell you how to go about helping your child in his social adjustment, only you are able to do this. What I can give you are some directions in which to concentrate your efforts.

Work to get the other children on his side, rather than against him. Think first of your child and consider his feelings, not what you want. For example, if he is uncomfortable in a regular classroom situation, don't let your own feelings keep him out of a special class or even a special school, where he would be relieved of the pressure of competing with others who fit into the norm of "normal." He also would receive a better education in such an environment, because the teaching would be geared to his level of comprehension and needs.

Your best line of defense for your child is a reasonable frankness and honesty about his problems. This means not hiding the fact that he is handicapped because of a problem (in learning, or controlling his hyperactivity, or epilepsy, et cetera), but not telling everyone everything, either. His teachers and the school principal need to know more details than does the neighbor down the street who comes into contact with your child only occasionally, and explanations to children should be made in very simple terminology. It is amazing how very often people — children and adults — respond with sympathy and the desire to help when they are told enough of the truth for their understanding.

For example — both Mike and Danny are "minimally brain-damaged," live in the same neighborhood, and are about the same age. Both have trouble controlling their actions and emotions and have some learning problems. Mike is the neighborhood brat and bully, not liked at all by the other children; Danny is a sweet child, accepted by the other children, and his sometimes erratic behavior is accepted by them as being just part of the way he is. "Danny sometimes has trouble understanding, and he needs our help," but "Mike is just mean and bad," I've heard the children say. Mike's mother insists, "Nothing is wrong with him except that the kids are always picking on him and blaming him for what they do." She isn't trusted because she will invariably find some way of placing the blame for Mike's misbehavior on another child even in the face of indisputable evidence to the contrary. Danny's mother has explained her son's problems to the neighbors, even relating some of their efforts to find help for him and what is being done at the present. "Please give him a chance," she asks. She explained to the children, "I know Danny can act bad at times, but there is a reason — he has a sort of broken connection in his thinking. Because he isn't able to do all the things you can do, this sometimes causes a short circuit in the way he acts." This is neither an exact nor a completely true explanation, but it is simple and enough for the children to understand that they are not responsible for his actions, nor will they be held responsible for Danny's misdeeds.

One season I watched the boys in the neighborhood work for hours and days on end to teach Danny how to play baseball. Mike was never included in their games, and once I asked why. "Because he always wants his own way, and whenever we tell him to wait his turn or play by the rules, he runs home to his mother and then she comes out yelling at us to stop picking on him."

I then asked, "What do you do when Danny wants his own way?"

"Oh, we just explain to him that he has to play by the rules. Sometimes we have to get rough with him and tell him to cool off before he can play, though."

A few weeks after this conversation, one of the boys told me, "Say, you know, Danny's really learned to hit the ball, and, boy, can he run!"

This is but a brief and simple resumé of the details of the two cases, and nothing has been said about the basic personality of the two boys, but the main difference is in the way the parents have chosen to handle their relationship with society. When Danny's parents explained enough of his problems to the neighbors and asked for their help, assuring them that no one would be expected to be responsible for his actions, their child was received and treated with sympathy and forgiveness.

Appearance — Personal Hygiene and Dress Clothes never made the man, but the condition of his clothes and his habits of personal hygiene are rather valid measures of what he thinks of himself. I know — when a child is extremely handicapped, to the extent perhaps that he must spend much of his day lying down, it often seems a waste of time to change him out of his night clothes into day clothes. Or, if no one but you is going to see him, why bother to put on diaper covers? But keeping him appropriately dressed in neat, clean clothes *is* important, because he then learns that he is important as a person. The significance isn't just the clothes, but the attitude that motivates your action. You must show your child that you have pride in him and that you believe he is truly important.

Little else can turn people off as much as a child who drools. Many types of handicapping conditions affect the swallowing muscles, resulting in uncontrolled drooling. In time and with speech therapy, many children overcome this, but in some instances it is just part of the handicap and cannot be over-come. Then drooling must be accepted and ways found to make it as unobtrusive as possible — keeping tissues or handker-chiefs close by, teaching him to wipe his own chin, or using bibs.

Your Child's Need for Responsibility　Teaching a child who is handicapped that he is a full-fledged member of his family is important for his development of self-esteem, especially if there are other children in the family. He sees his siblings per-forming their chores, and if he is not given some duties for which he is responsible, he may feel that he is not as important as they are. Sound far-fetched to you? Not at all. The real purpose of giving children chores is not to make the parents' life easier (it is all too often more wearying and time-consum-ing to make sure that they do their work), but to teach the children responsibility and dependability. Your handicapped child also needs to be given the opportunity to learn these character traits. Helping to sort the laundry or to take the clothes to the proper room is not too difficult a task for many children. Setting the table teaches him to count and to im-prove his eye-hand coordination as well as learn responsibility. Consider what your child is capable of doing and give him some task for which he is to be responsible. Just remember to start small and simple and then to insist that he is solely responsible for doing this, that no one else is going to do it for him.

Among other family responsibilities is that of sharing the parents' time with brothers and sisters. Although their need is not as obvious as is your handicapped child's, the other children in the family also deserve their parents' time and attention. Even if there are no other children in your family, some time must be reserved for yourself and for spending with your husband. Don't let your child be all-demanding of your attention. Remember that home life is also a training ground for his life and experiences outside the home.

Provide opportunities for your child to give of himself to others in the family. Children are basically selfish; learning to consider others is a learned response, not a natural one. Small deeds of thoughtfulness and consideration in addition to gift-giving must not be overlooked with your handicapped child.

Mothers Who Are Alone

Although what has been said in this chapter is directed primarily to mothers who share responsibility for their handicapped children with their husbands, most also applies to mothers who are alone, for the basic principles of good motherhood still apply.

In most aspects of her life, the mother who is raising her handicapped child alone is in a situation similar to that of all mothers alone — the same feeling of loneliness; the same, often overwhelming, parental responsibilities. There are some differences, however. Single mothers of handicapped children often are lonelier, and their parental responsibilities often are greater. Older nonhandicapped children usually can make many decisions for themselves; handicapped children often cannot and are much more dependent upon their mothers; child care for a young nonhandicapped child is easier to arrange so that his mother can work at a job, while satisfactory child care for a handicapped child very often is extremely difficult to arrange. Also, just taking care of a handicapped child at home is usually much more difficult than is looking after the needs of a nonhandicapped child.

For any mother alone, her life undergoes a drastic change, whether she is alone because of divorce or because of death. Not only does she no longer have a husband to share family responsibilities, but she must usually find some way of earning a wage, and so cannot stay at home to be a full-time mother. Consequently, making arrangements for child care is often the first step to be taken. Perhaps there are family members, such as grandparents, who can and are willing to look after the child; perhaps reliable household help can be found or a suitable child care center. Great, but such ideal arrangements are the exception rather than the rule. More often, the mother must move to a new location to find the right facilities. A solution many mothers have settled on is boarding school for their handicapped children, and in many instances this seems to be the best arrangement for all concerned. (A full discussion is given in the last chapter about residential facilities.)

The single mothers with whom I have spoken have all stressed one warning: remarriage is not necessarily the best solution. And, when considering such a decision, be sure that the child's stepfather-to-be understands the added responsibilities of a handicapped child in the family. (But does this not apply to any mother alone?)

Another word of advice several mothers mentioned concerns the father's responsibility to his child. If there is any communication between the mother and father, and particularly if he shows any interest in his child's progress and welfare, do allow him to share in part of the decision-making — especially if the decisions concern schooling or boarding facilities for which he will be expected to share in the expense. This is a father's right, and by allowing him to help plan his child's future, the mother is relieved of some of her burden of responsibility. (This will not suit every family, of course, but I believe it is advice well worth considering.)

Mothers who are alone do not have to remain lonely. Because there are so many other mothers who are also alone, sympathetic companionship can be found usually without too much difficulty. Those of you who are alone know that while sympathy is easy for the mother of a handicapped child to find, all too often finding real understanding and constructive empathy is difficult. One of the most valuable resources of constructive help and understanding is parents' groups, especially if your child is at home. Listed in the Appendix are some organizations concerned with handicapped children and their parents. The national offices also function as information and referral sources for locating local chapters. In groups such as Parents Without Partners, you will find others who understand the problems you are facing. Understanding is important, but the real purpose of belonging to such groups is that by being among people who have experienced similar situations, you will also find answers to your own questions and solutions which can be applied to your own problems. You will need to draw on many resources to find the encouragement that will strengthen your self-confidence and hope for the future.

My heart goes out to those of you who are alone. Having a child who is handicapped is difficult enough to cope with when the father is present in the home; to be alone must require a tremendous amount of strength of personality and resolve.

Summary

Being a good mother to a child who is handicapped isn't really so difficult and not really so very different from just being a mother. Every child has unique needs to be met in unique ways. Just keep in mind that your handicapped child is a child first and foremost. Because of his deficiency, certain adaptations and alterations must be made in your daily life and the methods you use to train and teach him to develop that ability which he does have. Although each child has needs different from other children, all have the same basic need — to be loved and accepted as they are. Feel free to love your child and acceptance will follow naturally.

Keep these general goals and you will satisfactorily fulfill your role as mother: (1) work toward maintaining a balance of enough and not too much in all you do; (2) be natural and realize that you are not superhuman; and (3) don't be afraid that you are incapable of doing your job of caring for this child. Remember that inside all of us there is a limitless fountain of strength, an ever-flowing well of love. The troubles arise when outside influences and pressures cause a wall to be built around these strengths. Have confidence in yourself — you *are* capable, and you *can* do it!

5. You Are Important Too

YOUR ROLE AS WIFE has been discussed, and your role as mother has been analyzed, now what about you as yourself? You are important, too, and at the very apex of this triangle of your role responsibility is your responsibility to yourself. Your success as a wife and as a mother depends to a great extent upon what you are as a person — how well you meet and overcome adversity, your determination to keep going despite setbacks, your willingness to exert the effort necessary to turn challenge into achievement, and your ability to see the happiness in your life rather than dwell on the sadness. Your happiness does not rely upon your child, or upon your husband, but upon you. You hold your happiness in *your* hand; it lies within your heart.

Although your capacity for happiness (self-satisfaction, contentment, fulfillment, call it what you like) is inherent to your personality, it is not going to come to the forefront unassisted. With your will power you must force your mind to break down the walls of your discontent. Each time you look squarely at an incident of misfortune and tell yourself, "I'm not going to let this defeat me," you will gain in strength; each time you give in to self-pity, you will lose strength and defeat will then come closer.

You cannot forget that you are important. You are a person in your own right, a separate identity who also has needs to be satisfied, weaknesses to be strengthened, and demands to be met. For many of these you can depend only upon yourself, for only you are able to really understand how you feel, and you most often are the best judge of what it is you need.

Expanding Your Inner Strength

How do you develop your inner strength? First, don't ever say "I can't," for that is the first step toward defeat. At the same time, keep your goal-achievement expectation down to a reasonable level. You are not all-powerful, you are only human. But you can say "I'll try."

Second, look for practical solutions to your problems. Very often the solutions are simple and lie right under your nose. Don't be afraid to substitute alternate plans or even to completely change the direction of your actions.

Third, don't expect to solve everything at once. You've a mountain of problems ahead of you to solve, but only a few need to be solved today. If you learn to take one step at a time, one problem at a time, when you reach that "mountain," you will find it is not there. Learn, too, how to discern the problems that should be solved immediately, and those that are unimportant and should be laid aside for a while. Time has a way of mellowing even the most difficult problems, others dissolve as time passes, and still others grow smaller and less difficult as you grow and learn. This doesn't mean, however, that you have free rein to run away from your problems — you cannot shut the door of your mind and pretend there is no problem — rather, that you don't try to work everything out immediately. Learn to be patient.

Fourth, don't let your mistakes get you down; learn to profit by the errors in judgment you will surely make. You will make mistakes, and even your best thought-out decisions will sometimes be erroneous. You can never rectify some mistakes completely, but you will grow in wisdom if you can learn from them.

Go in search of help, just as you did when you opened the cover to this book and began to read the first page. There are many sources of help you can utilize. Only the foolish man (or woman) says "I don't need anyone. I can do it all by myself." The wise ones take advantage of every source of information and help they can find. After you've gathered information, weighed and considered counsel and advice, then you will have tools to use in making your decisions.

Hand in hand with these steps are other approaches helpful in strengthening your capability to manage. Do let your religious faith work for you. Here is an ever-present source of strength and guidance, and I hope with all my heart that you have some degree of faith — or that those of you who do not will find it.

Think positively; tell yourself you are strong. Analyze your motives and your motivations, taking careful account of your strong and your weak areas. While you'll not be able to analyze yourself perfectly, this self-evaluation will uncover many sides of your personality that are positive and will reveal other facets that need improving.

Does it seem I am giving a character analysis of a paragon of wisdom, intelligence, and strong will power? That is *exactly* my intention! For that is the ideal toward which you strive. This is the goal you set yourself.

But, at the same time, don't set your expectations too high — learn how to bend with the wind. There are going to be times when you will not be able to fight a particular adversity, when your best action is nonaction. There will be other occasions when you will just have to go along with some change because you can do nothing about it.

Your Need for Professional Guidance   Seeking the advice and counsel of people trained and experienced in the professions concerning mental and emotional health has been mentioned before, but your need for reassurance and guidance never vanishes. The causes of your need and your questions change as time alters your situation. The problems you will have when your child is ten years old, for example, are quite different from those which confronted you when he was an infant and will be different when he becomes an adolescent. You, also, pass through stages of development when your own needs differ.

Don't be afraid that you are revealing weakness of character when you ask for guidance — you are just being smart enough to realize that someone else may have a better answer or can point out a plan of action that you are unaware of or have not considered.

You Can Learn to Help Yourself Outside sources of help are valuable and necessary, but you must also be concerned with ways in which you can help yourself answer your own questions. You live with this situation everyday, and even with all the outside help you may receive, it is still up to you to apply what you learn to yourself. Your adjustment is your responsibility, one that no one else can do for you.

You can resolve to look for what is good in your life rather than letting your thoughts dwell on your misfortune, but only you can put that resolve into action. Reassurance will be offered you by others, and because you need all the reassurance you are given, do not turn your back on praise and encouragement. But, you cannot live successfully upon praise of others, you must learn to value your own ability and strength.

Job-holding Working outside the home is the solution many mothers have found for developing their self-confidence and self-esteem. For some, this is excellent therapy. Holding down a job outside the home can relieve many pressures — financial, overconcern about the child and his developmental progress, being denied association with people, and boredom. Just being away from the constant demands of a handicapped child for a few hours a day can restore a mother's sense of equilibrium and perspective. Being paid to do something can also be a valuable aid in strengthening one's sense of self-worth and pride.

A woman's decision to work outside her home or not should be considered in the light of her entire situation — what her interests are and how she feels she can best use her particular talents, the needs of her family, and how her husband feels about her working. In making this decision, as in making so many others, listen to your heart, for only if your actions satisfy your inner needs and drives will you be truly fulfilled and happy. Even if the decision is prompted by financial needs, the decision is still yours alone to make.

The Wide World of Volunteer Service   If you feel you are not quite ready to tackle the job market, consider the wide range of volunteer services. Any contribution which you make will be valuable to some segment of society and will meet some need that would otherwise not be met. Your service will be beneficial to you also, providing you with experience and training and giving you that all-important satisfaction of being able to do something to help someone else. Regardless of the extent of your talents, training, or education, you have something of value to donate toward meeting the needs of others less fortunate than you. Indeed, our society would be in very sad condition were it not for the many thousands of women who donate millions of hours toward helping others. If you look around, you will realize that it is these unpaid workers who really provide the oil that keeps the machinery of society running smoothly.

There is one area of volunteer service for which you are particularly qualified — the organizations for parents who have handicapped children. Parents' groups have formed a most instrumental body in arousing public concern about the needs of handicapped children. Because of the interest stirred up and kept aflame by these groups, effective legislation has been passed for the improved welfare, education, and training of children handicapped by all types of deficiencies. From some of the educational methods developed for teaching mentally retarded children, improved methods for teaching have been developed, so all children have benefited from what was originally designed to help those who were below average in learning ability. Research into the causes and treatment of deficiencies which handicap children has led to discoveries that improve the health of all children.

Do Not Shortchange Your Family   Now, don't become so involved in performing services to help others that you shortchange your own family. Escaping for a few hours from the demands of your family is good relaxation and often necessary for maintaining equilibrium of concern. But be careful that escape doesn't become running away, that meeting others' needs does not become more important to you than meeting the needs of your own family. This is warning of a very real and possible danger. Even mothers involved with helping other handicapped children may be guilty of this. Don't let your child be like the shoemaker's children who were shoeless, as happened with one family I know.

The parents were young, wealthy, and community-spirit-minded. Because they could afford to hire a nurse-governess for their deaf daughter, the mother was free to work toward improving the lot of other deaf children in her community. She organized an educational program designed especially for deaf children and founded a clinic to care for deaf children in the lower economic group. All in all, she was responsible for a tremendous number of good accomplishments for the improved welfare of deaf children. All very well and good, but in her concern and efforts to help others, she neglected her own daughter. Deprived of her mother's time and concern, she felt denied of her love and became unhappy, withdrawn, insecure, and unable to develop her own high potential. Eventually, after rather extensive psychiatric therapy and counseling for the family, the daughter regained emotional stability, and perhaps just in time, her mother realized how much her daughter needed to know her love. Much unhappiness could have been avoided had she been aware of this earlier and balanced her outside activities with her family responsibility.

Summary

Sometimes as you think about your responsibilities to your husband and your child, the task of trying to satisfy their need for you seems to be just too much, doesn't it? You are not alone in feeling this way; listen to these mothers talk about their feelings.

"I feel as if I'm all alone, trying to pull a gigantic load across a wilderness."

"I am not superwoman, and yet that is just what I think I'm expected to be."

"I feel so unimportant, so insignificant. When do I come in for some consideration?"

A group of mothers whose children were handicapped talking? No, this was a conversation among mothers whose children had not one deficiency that we could term a handicap.

While your life as mother and wife is basically similar to the way it would have been if your child were not handicapped, the very fact that he is means that different emphasis is placed upon certain aspects of these roles for you. Because having a child who is handicapped is a totally unexpected circumstance, you feel you are unprepared to meet the challenge; as you try to look into the uncharted years ahead, you believe yourself to be ill-equipped and lacking in the strength you know you will need to have. You are no different from anyone else in feeling this way. If any person, regardless of ability, endowment, or whatever, could be given a glimpse into his future, he would quail at the thought of having to face those problems he would see ahead of him. Reality has been brought closer for you, and the future problems are in clearer focus now. It is no wonder you doubt your ability and your strength. You would not be human if you did not — and certainly you'd not be honest with yourself.

But, you do have the ability, you do have the strength you

will need, for this is a basic part of your personality. To let yourself believe you are weak and incapable is to be defeated before you even have a chance to fight. True, some women do seem to have more will, more resolve, and more ability than others, but deep within the core of her personality, *every* woman has more strength than she may realize. Strength lies in the ability to look beneath the surface feelings of inadequacies and fears so inner resources can be recognized and brought to light.

The difficult-to-define or -describe "strength of character," which is so necessary a personality trait for you, must be developed by *you*. Others can and will help and encourage you, and they will pick you up when you fall, but this growing and maturing (for that is what it is really all about) is your own responsibility.

You must develop and expand your self-confidence. Go in search of ways to use your abilities, and you will then find reason for pride in yourself. Use your talents in helping others, and you will find new purpose in your life. Learn how to rest and relax, for your emotions, your mind, and your body need periods of recuperation in order to function effectively. Don't set standards of competence or goals of achievement that are too high for you to attain realistically; just convince yourself that you will be defeated by no adversity.

When your head says "I can't," listen closely, you will hear your heart faintly saying "I will find a way. I can."

6. Especially for Husbands

WHATEVER THE CAUSE of a child's handicap, whether his deficiency is mental or physical or a combination, this is a catastrophe that inevitably causes stress and strain upon his parents' marriage. Every nuance of the relationship between husband and wife is affected in some respect, and differences and disagreements which may otherwise have been overlooked in importance can become major causes of incompatability. Whether the child's deficiency is relatively minor or recognizably major, his parents' reactions to his handicap can make this an adversity capable of destroying their marriage.

These are strong terms, I know, but the marriage mortality rate among parents of handicapped children is very high. Being alerted to the reality of the dangers, perhaps you will then be aware of the necessity of finding effective measures to protect your own marriage.

Now, while it is certainly true that unusual strains will be exerted on your marriage because your child is handicapped, there is another side to the coin; this circumstance can be an instrument whereby the bonds of love between you and your wife are strengthened, and your relationship developed to levels of great meaningfulness and satisfaction.

The very fact that both of you are so deeply affected by what has happened to your child increases your need for each other. If each of you strives to understand the other so you can respond effectively to the other's needs, your love will deepen and mature. By working together and uniting your efforts to overcome the effects of your child's handicap, you will learn to respect each other's unique qualities of strength and capability. Because you share your love, concern, and responsibility for this child who needs both of you so much, you will also share the heart-break of failure and the joy of success, and this sharing can draw you into closer communion with each other.

All of this will not just happen naturally, however. Achieving this quality in a marriage requires an exertion of effort by both husband and wife. Each must be willing to lay self-concern aside and put concern for the other first. Each must learn to resolve feelings of blame and resentment toward the other. Both must learn the value of offering encouragement and sense when consolation is needed. Although your wife has her own responsibilities in the strengthening and development of your marriage relationship, your responsibility is just as great. Without your cooperation, her efforts will be futile.

The following chapter is neither a treatise on "how to be a good husband," nor is it a "marriage manual." Rather, hints and clues will be given that will aid you in understanding your wife and her reactions to the fact that your child is handicapped, so you will better know how to respond to her need for you. Some of this discussion may not fit your situation at all, other parts you may only think do not apply to you, and some you will recognize fit you and your marriage like a glove. None is offered as a cure-all, but rather as mind-openers so you can then go ahead on your own to find the solutions to your par-ticular problems.

Right now, you may think that the challenge is too great for you to meet, but it isn't — not if you are willing to learn to listen to your heart and then be guided by your own inner strength and goodness. Remember also, you are not fighting this battle of adjustment alone — your wife is there beside you, and together you will strengthen each other. Each parent must develop personal strength and courage, but successful acceptance and adjustment is a two-parent, cooperative endeavor toward which both parents strive to contribute their best efforts of helping each other.

Understanding Your Wife's Reactions

While your wife has many of the same reactions to your child's being handicapped as you have, because she is a woman and mother, some of her reactions are quite different. By understanding how she feels and why, you will then have an insight into her needs and how you can help her find and develop the strength for her acceptance and adjustment.

Now, understanding how your wife is affected by what has happened to your child is necessary and important, but don't become so concerned about her as the mother of your handicapped child that you forget she is first and foremost your wife. In many respects you will help her most by letting her know she comes first in your thoughts and consideration and by giving her no reason to doubt your love of her. Also, if you show her you respect her as a person, and that you believe she is capable of being a good mother and coping with the problems, she will then be free to develop her own strength and to become the wife you need and the mother your child needs.

Your Wife's Guilt-Imps If your child's handicap is a result of an illness or accident, your wife may feel she is more directly to blame than you are, because as mother the responsibility of child care is predominantly hers. When the handicap is the result of a birth injury or a prenatal mishap, because the baby is nurtured and develops inside the woman's body, a mother often feels almost totally responsible for the condition of the child she produces.

Unresolved guilt can undermine your wife's efforts to accept her child as being handicapped, to adjust her approach to life in the light of having an imperfect child. Certainly, guilt can hinder her realization of the full potential she has as a capable person in her own right to be a good wife and mother.

Now, insofar as her guilt is concerned, what your wife needs from you, the person whose opinion of her she values most, is reassurance that she was not at fault, that there were extenuating circumstances over which she had no control which were the basic causes. She also needs the reassurance from you that you do not blame her, that she has not done anything that would lessen your love for and respect of her. One of the surest methods of destroying all shreds of self-reassurance your wife may have been successful in maintaining is to let her think you hold her responsible for what has happened to your child.

Your wife is fighting her own battle against her guilt, and she needs your encouragement to be strong enough to overcome her self-blame. Talk to her, tell her you understand (even if you really don't yet). Make her believe that you see hidden reserves of her will power, capability, and strength. Let her know, too, that you will be there to support her when she needs your strength to bolster her own.

Again, *never,* by words or by actions, so much as hint that you harbor even the slightest feelings of blame toward your wife. She is having a hard enough time as it is resolving her guilt; forcing her to defend herself against your accusations can be too much for her. Talk to someone else whom you trust, your minister or rabbi or your doctor, if you feel you cannot reveal your thoughts to a friend. (Perhaps you feel it is wrong not to be honest with her about how you feel. Maybe blaming her is being dishonest with yourself?)

Your Wife and Her Grief   Again, speaking in terms that apply to the basic differences between women and men, your wife feels grief just as you do because her child is imperfect, but her child's need of her as mother tends to lessen the intensity of her grief. Because she knows she must respond to her child's need of her and, therefore, cannot let her grief affect her ability to care for him, she may conceal her feelings behind a facade of calm and logical thinking while all the time her heart is breaking behind an icy wall of remorse. She needs your understanding of her reactions so she will be able to find the strength she must have to absolve her grief. (Some women, of course, are never able to overcome their grief, never able to turn their attention away from themselves and what they have lost to focus on their children and their needs and on what they have not lost. Guilt and hostility often are the feelings that prompt continued grief.)

Most women have built-in defenses against the ravages of grief, such as an innate desire to console and to respond to being needed. Because of this, before your words of understanding and consolation can be effective for your wife, she must not only know that you understand that she is grieving, but also that you need her consolation of you in your grief. In other words, you must accept her efforts to respond to your need of her.

Let me relate an example of how *not* to handle grief. Sue and Bob lost their only daughter. Neither was at fault — on her way home from school little Mary was hit by a delivery truck when she darted into the street to pick up a book she had dropped. She died instantly. The death of their daughter was a shattering tragedy for both parents, but Sue accepted the consolation offered her by friends and relatives and was then able to find the strength she needed to control her grief. Being able to cope with her own grief, she could then turn to responding to their two sons' need of her and to helping them find ways of coping with their grief. Bob would not accept Sue's attempts to console him and allowed no one else to reach him in consolation. Bound up in his own self-concern and grief, he made no attempt to help his sons or Sue through their ordeals.

Several years have now passed, and although Sue still grieves for her daughter, Mary's death no longer casts a shadow on her life. Bob is almost losing grips with his life because he has continued to live under the shadow of his unresolved grief, which has now grown out of all proportion to reality. The family should have been drawn closer together because of this tragedy, but instead they were torn apart. Bob has alienated himself from his sons, and the misunderstanding between Sue and Bob has grown into a barrier which now threatens to destroy their marriage. The difference between the quality of their adjustment lies not so much with their different personalities (although that is always a predominant factor), but with the fact that Sue accepted consolation for her grief, and in being able then to turn her attention away from herself to meet her sons' need of her, she found answers to her own questions.

Grief held inside and not shared only grows in intensity; not responding to another's need for consolation provides the nourishment upon which self-grief grows.

Understanding a Mother's Disappointment   Your wife also feels the pangs of disappointment that her child will not be as she had expected, but her disappointment is often for different broken dreams than yours. A father may assume that his disappointment is greater than his wife's because he feels his dreams were for more important goals — the carrying on of the family name and traditions, the anticipation of achievements his son would have accomplished, his daughter's fulfillment as a woman successfully exemplifying the quality of his fatherhood and his own concepts of the male-female relationship, for instance. Because his dreams were "big," a father may feel that his wife's disappointment should be less intense, for her dreams were "less important." But this is not a valid line of reasoning — a mother's disappointment is just as logical as a father's.

A mother's disappointment more often is concerned with what she is denied in her role as mother. Denials such as these perhaps summarize your wife's disappointment. Now she will not be able to share the many facets of womanhood with her daughter as she guides her growth from child to woman; she may never be able to teach her daughter to cook or comb her hair or learn the ground rules for dressing stylishly and attractively. It may be that she will not have the opportunity to realize the fullness of the role of mother to her son in small yet important ways, such as bandaging the knees he surely would have skinned when learning to skate and ride a bicycle; or watching him play baseball with the team; or even fearfully watching him climb the big tree in the backyard. If your child's handicap is mental, your wife, too, suffers deep disappointment because of the pleasure and pride she is denied because of her child's lack of ability to achieve the usually expected accomplishments.

Small reasons to feel disappointment so acutely? Not at all, for it is the small, everyday challenges and rewards that comprise the backbone of the fulfillment of motherhood.

How do you help your wife cope with her disappointment? Let her know you understand her feelings of disappointment and that you respect her reasons for feeling as she does. Help her understand that none of the basic aspects of motherhood will be denied her, but only that the fulfillment of her role will be in ways different from those she had expected and anticipated; that she will not be denied the opportunity of being mother to this child because he is handicapped.

Your Wife's Fear-Imps Apprehension and periods of even actual fear are expected parts of being a mother — indeed, of being a parent. However, a handicapped child's lack of ability increases his mother's sense of responsibility for him, and so the emphasis of her concern is altered and her fear is often more intense. Because unrelieved apprehension can eventually grow into panic so overwhelming that the ability for effective action is destroyed, it is very important that your wife overcome her fears — and to do this, she needs your help.

Your particular situation and your wife's individual personality will, of course, determine how you can best help her, but to know what she needs of you, you must have some understanding of the causes of her fears. As you try to understand how your wife feels, remember that because the responsibilities of her role as mother differ from yours as father, so will her apprehension and fear arise from different causes. In other words — her fear-imps often are different from those fears which plague you.

Underlying your wife's other fears is fear that she will not be capable of being a good mother to her child because he is handicapped. Her anxiety about her ability to be his mother ranges from the day-to-day responsibilities of caring for his needs and teaching him to those vaguely understood greater responsibilities that lie in the future. At times she may be afraid that she is unable to love this child who demands so much of her — especially after a day when nothing she has done for him seems to have been successful. She may look ahead and see only unrewarding repetition of her present life with her child; she may wonder if her resentment of him because of his handicap and the problems caused by his lack of ability will eventually destroy her love for him.

Overdeveloped fear that something else will happen to her handicapped child can result in a mother's overprotective attitude. She may become afraid to leave him alone even for a short period of time, afraid to leave him in anyone else's care, even afraid to let him sleep in his own room at night. An overprotective attitude can also cause a mother to be afraid for her own safety, overcautious to the extreme of being afraid even to leave her home. "Suppose something should happen to me and I wouldn't be able to take care of my child — who would look after him then?"

These may seem to be extreme examples, but they do occur. A reasonable caution is necessary, of course, but overcaution is unhealthy for the child, prohibitive of his growth and development, and detrimental for his parents. Fearfulness which leads to a mother's overprotection often is a result of her feeling that she is totally responsible for her child. By sharing some of the responsibility for your child — his exercises, decisions about treatment and therapy, even feeding and bathing him sometimes — you can relieve your wife of much of the burden of responsibility she carries and perhaps also relieve much of her fear that she is unable to manage.

Most fathers suffer periods when they are afraid they are unable to provide financial security for their families, and the financial burdens incurred when a child is handicapped are justifiable causes for fear. Wives worry about finances, too, but their financial fears often stem from different causes. For instance, a wife worries about whether or not she will be competent in managing the money her husband provides and about what she would do if something should happen to him or to his earning ability. At times she may even fear that she will be unable to be the kind of wife her husband needs for the development of his ability to achieve success in his work. A wife's own security is threatened, too, because of the financial burdens of having a handicapped child.

Keeping your wife informed of your plans for future financial security, such as life insurance, investments, retirement benefits, et cetera, does much to relieve her fears about the future. Soft-pedaling your complaints to your wife about the lack of money, insecurity of your job, and so on also helps to lessen the pressure of financial worries for her. Certainly your wife deserves your honesty concerning the state of the family financial situation, since she must have this knowledge if she is to adjust her spending, but don't make her a constant sounding board for your own worries. You must feel free to discuss your job frustrations with your wife and sometimes your financial worries, for this is the kind of honesty which is necessary for a truly happy marriage relationship — just be careful not to overdo it.

These are only a few of the fear-imps which plague mothers, and having a handicapped child only provides more causes to intensify a mother's fears. Because you are her husband, you are the person closest to her, and because you have an intimate knowledge of the situation, there is much you can do to help her fight her fears. Listen to what she says and pay attention to the meaning that may lie behind her words. Let her feel free to confide in you her feelings of fear and apprehension with no sense of being judged by you. Be aware, too, of the importance of pointing out her successes to her, for it is all too easy to see only one's mistakes and be fearful of future failures. Do not tell her that she is foolish to be so afraid for your child or of the awesome demands and responsibilities of the future — reassure her that she possesses the capabilities needed to cope with the problems. Above all, give her the security of knowing that you are there with her. Be ready to understand and to support her, to ease her burden of responsibility — to love her.

Resentment is Natural Even though your wife knows in her heart that resenting her child is wrong, that to resent the fact that her child is handicapped is but a negative reaction which may make her adjustment harder, this is one emotional reaction which will arise from time to time — just as it does for every mother. Your wife is perfectly within her rights to feel as she does, and she has more reason than other mothers may have to resent this child because of the demands his handicapping deficiency places on her.

It is only natural that she resent being so tied down at home because she cannot take her child out with her, or because competent baby sitters are difficult to find or to pay for out of the budget. It is only human that she resent at times the extra work she must do because of her child's handicap. Or, if she had to give up a job she enjoyed and which gave her a sense of successful personal achievement, it is only natural that she feel resentment, because her drive for personal accomplishment seems now to be thwarted.

The list of causes for a mother's resentment is endless, but these are feelings which most mothers experience at one time or another, especially when their children are young. However, the mother whose child is not handicapped knows that her mother-responsibilities will decrease and change and that the time will come when she will again be free to pursue her own goals of achievement.

A woman's whole pattern of life is changed when she has a handicapped child. No longer can she look forward to a natural sequence of changing responsibility toward her child as he moves from one level of growth and development to the next; no longer can she anticipate the time when she would be free to pursue some of her own interests and goals; no longer can she anticipate the same satisfaction of achievement as a mother that she had expected. In such a situation it is difficult for a woman *not* to resent the course her life has been forced to take because of her handicapped child.

Resentment is a natural way for your wife to react, and she is only being very human to feel as she does. Do not be angry with her or lose your respect for her — understand that the causes for her resentment are very real and very reasonable. Sympathize with her, and let her know that you do.

Summary Having a child who is handicapped places a tremendous strain on the relationship between parents. To overcome the ill effects this strain invariably causes in the marriage, both parents must keep in mind their responsibility to each other. Love is vitally necessary to a good marriage as is respect for each other and concern for each other's happiness. In a good marriage husband and wife work together to overcome their adversities, and it is through this sense of unity, of togetherness, that they develop then the strength to withstand the pressures and solve their problems.

To develop this sense of unity, each must be aware of the needs of the other for him, as well as each one's need for freedom and encouragement in order to reach toward the development of capabilities and the strengthening of character. This necessary awareness and encouragement cannot be possible unless there is understanding of the motivations which prompt the need. Understanding will not just come naturally, there must be the will to exert the effort.

Because your wife's role as mother is different from yours as father, many of her feelings concerning having a child who is handicapped will be different from your own. Some of her emotional reactions you will be able to understand and accept easily; others will be hard for you to consider as being even vaguely logical — but what man ever really understood a woman? (Indeed, what person can ever completely understand another?) Understanding is important, but you must also simply accept some of her feelings, giving her credit as a person that her actions and reactions are prompted by reasonable motivations, and you must respect these motivations.

More than anyone else, you can help your wife accept the fact of your child's deficiency and find the necessary strength she must have to adjust her life; more than anyone else, yours is the responsibility to do so. Being a good husband is not just providing material security for your wife, it is also giving her the security of knowing you love her and that you respect her as a competent person. Her ability to accept the reality of your child's handicap and to adjust her life pattern accordingly will be less effective if she feels your love for her has weakened; her ability will be strengthened by your assurances of love.

Part of this assurance is giving her encouragement when her resolve falters and part is being supportive to her at those times when her strength has weakened. Part of this reassurance also is respecting her ability and innate strength as she strives to develop the inner resources of her own personality.

All this will not be as difficult as you may think, for if you will let your love and compassion for your wife guide your thinking, you will then be free to listen to your heart, and you will be directed by the essence of your own inner strength and goodness to understand her.

The Husband-to-Wife Relationship

The quality of your relationship with your wife determines (and is also determined by) how effectively you can help her in her efforts to accept and adjust to the fact that your child is handicapped. This is a situation which has a permanent effect on both of you and your marriage; and because each of you has been so deeply affected, your need of each other is greater now. Therefore, you both must exert extra effort to build a relationship which is meaningful and satisfying to each.

Strengthening and improving the quality of your relationship is a continual and continuing endeavor, and while every marriage is unique there are certain aspects which are common to the success of any marriage.

The Importance of Good Communication   The ability to communicate with each other is an absolute necessity if your marriage is to be happy and satisfying. (Communication is defined in *The American Heritage Dictionary* as: "to have an interchange of thoughts or ideas.") You will be able to help your wife in her adjustment only if the level of communication between you is good, for you must know what her needs are before you can respond effectively.

The most important way of communicating is through conversation. In the intimate relationship of marriage conversation takes on a deeper meaning, encompassing understanding of and respect for feelings and opinions; it means freedom to converse openly about one's worries, hopes and dreams, frustrations and guilts without fear of censure. It is through oral communication that information is exchanged, consolation offered, and hope is strengthened.

For conversation to be real communication, one must not just listen to the words, but hear the meaning the words convey, react to and perceive the thoughts and feelings the words express. Developing communication that is meaningful and satisfying involves being honest, not just being truthful — and there is a difference. Honest is being sincere about one's feelings; truthful is carefully relating the facts. The difference is slight, but while one cannot be honest without being truthful, one can be truthful without being honest. To be honest is to go that one step further and reveal how one feels in response to the facts.

Don't underestimate your wife's need for communication (conversation) with you. She has problems that need your help in solving; she needs your support and reassurance that what she is doing is right, and there are times when her line of thinking should be redirected. She also needs just simple, adult, give-and-take conversation with you, especially if she must spend most of her time alone at home. She needs interchange of information that will help her relate to the world outside her home — and sometimes, to *your* world outside the home and family.

If you don't talk with her and listen to what she says, your wife will begin to feel that you don't consider her important or that you think she isn't intelligent enough to understand. If she feels she cannot converse with you, she will be forced to keep her feelings bottled up inside and eventually she may explode in rage or find someone else who will listen to her.

"All right, so it's important to talk with my wife," you may agree, "but when? I'm tired when I come home from work and she's busy. There's too much to do on the weekends. When is there time to talk?"

The answer — you make the time. Set aside a definite time each day just for the two of you, to be interrupted or canceled only for reasons of emergency. Even fifteen minutes can be sufficient, although at least thirty minutes is more reasonable. In addition to the daily time-alone, if at all possible, reserve one evening a week just for the two of you. Although going out is best, this is not always possible. The same benefits can be received from an evening spent together at home, and even one night a month is better than none at all. If your wife should suggest such a time-alone, do go along with her proposal — but, if you take the initiative yourself, you will then give her a very special gift — the gift of knowing she is important to you.

The Importance of Confessed Love When a woman is a wife, much of her sense of security depends upon how sure she is that her husband loves her. Although a man may shower his wife with gifts, treat her with the utmost respect and consideration, and seldom criticize her, unless he tells her "I love you" in words, she has reason to doubt that he does.

Having a handicapped child increases a wife's dependency upon her husband in many ways. The frustrations of trying to cope with the extraordinary problems tend to threaten her feeling of security and to make her vulnerable to doubt that she is capable of functioning effectively in her roles as wife and mother. Because of all this, she needs even more assurance of her husband's love than perhaps she would need if there were no handicapped child in the family.

The words "I love you" are perhaps the three simplest words in the language, but they are the most important in marriage. These three little words imply many meanings, but essentially all connote, "You are important to me." In some unexplainable way, when a wife's world is out of kilter and she feels defeated in every endeavor, when her husband says to her, "I love you," she gains renewed strength to set her world back into proper balance, and insurmountable problems then shrink to a manageable size. So, hearing you say the actual words is extremely important to your wife, because you are assuring her of your love in a way that deeds cannot do.

Now, of course, words alone are not sufficient to prove to your wife you love her. Indeed, words without action appear false, for the mind not only listens to the heart, but also is influenced by visible and tangible proof of the speaker's sincerity. While it is logical that such considerations as fidelity and lack of physical or vocal abuse are evident proof of love and respect, there are many other less obvious, but not less important, ways by which a husband reassures his wife that he loves her. Many of these are the small, everyday gestures of thoughtfulness and consideration which also prove respect, and because they are such a part of the regular routine of life, are often so easily overlooked.

For example, a husband reinforces his words of love when he remembers to let his wife know he will be late for dinner; when he remembers her birthday and their anniversary; when he asks her opinion and then listens to her reply; when he compliments her for the meal she has cooked and praises her accomplishments, he tells her that she is important to him.

Gift-giving is another way of saying "I love you," and the gifts don't have to be expensive. A small gift, just because "this reminded me of you," is more precious to most wives than an expensive piece of jewelry purchased at the last minute to fulfill the obligation of a gift-giving occasion. It is the attitude of thoughtfulness that prompted the gift which is meaningful.

Love is important in any marriage, but when a child is handicapped it is vital that the love his parents feel for each other be strong. It is their love and the respect they feel for each other that is the most valuable asset for acceptance and adjustment.

Your Role as Lover   In perhaps no other aspect of marriage is the strain of having a handicapped child reflected more acutely than in the parents' sexual relationship. The physical relationship between husband and wife is often a barometer registering the atmosphere of their entire relationship to each other. Everything that happens in a marriage affects this relationship, and because a woman's physical responsiveness is greatly affected by what affects her emotionally, having a child who is handicapped influences her attitudes and responsiveness to sex in many ways which most men find hard to understand.

One such negative affect often felt by mothers in such circumstances is a lessening of the regard she feels for herself as a woman. (Frequently, the more serious the handicap, the greater the effect on the mother.) Actually, this is a very logical sequence of cause and effect. Because motherhood is such an integral part of womanhood, if a woman feels she has failed in her function as mother (by producing an imperfect child, or by not protecting her child from illness or injury), she may feel this indicates that she is not capable of being a complete woman with the ability to fulfill her role as wife.

The wise husband understands that this is an expected and natural way for his wife to react, and so he makes an effort to convince her that she has lost none of her womanly appeal for him, nor has she lost any of her capability to respond to him. He is patient, for he understands that his wife needs time to work out the many problems of her adjustment. He knows, too, that his praise and encouragement and consistent reaffirmation of his love for her will strengthen her efforts to help herself, and that criticism and disapproval will only weaken her resolve.

There are many other stresses that inhibit a mother's ability to respond sexually. One such stress is physical fatigue. Caring for a dependent child drains a mother's energy; a constant, day-in and day-out burden that can so completely exhaust her that she really has no strength left at the end of the day for lovemaking. Worry and concern about her responsibilities to her child can deplete a mother's store of emotional response, too. Understanding your wife's emotional and physical fatigue is important, but it is also necessary that you make an effort to relieve some of the causes by sharing the responsibilities and by lessening the burden of child care and other chores.

Fear of pregnancy can be another deterrent to a woman's responsiveness to lovemaking. I believe it is hard (if not absolutely impossible) for most men to comprehend the fear that a mother who has a handicapped child feels about having another child. It is a cold, sometimes almost paralyzing panic that can supersede all reasonable logic and knowledge. Fortunately, because of advances in medical knowledge, birth control today is easily managed. But don't place the responsibility entirely on your wife. Talk it over with her so you can then decide together on a method which is agreeable to both of you and physically safe for her.

This is certainly not a complete discussion of marital sexual adjustment, nor is it intended to be. These are just a few of the ways women are often affected by having a handicapped child. Sex is important to a marriage. It is the ultimate expression of the love that husband and wife feel for each other, and in many aspects, it is a crystallization of the quality of all their feelings for each other. There will inevitably be problems in your sexual relationship, for no marriage is completely free of misunderstandings, and because your child is handicapped, your marriage will be subjected to even greater problems. But in this aspect of your marriage as in others, you and your wife have an advantage which other couples often do not have — your need of each other is so great because of your child, both of you have added incentive to work together to develop your relationship into a good and lasting marriage that will strengthen each of you.

Boosting Your Wife's Self-Confidence   Another need your wife has of you is to be her confidence booster. You know from your own experiences how easily a sense of failure in one area of responsibility carries over into the other areas of responsibility, and that conviction of having failed can eventually so weaken a person's level of self-confidence that the will to attempt any sort of endeavor is stifled. You know, too, that sense of failure is greater when the area of responsibility is a major one — and motherhood is one such area for a woman even if she holds a full-time job outside her home. It is natural for a wife to look first to her husband for reassurance when she feels she has failed and to turn to him first for encouragement and reassurance that she is capable of trying again.

Just what is self-confidence? Most people have a general idea of the meaning, but the dictionary definition may help crystallize the concept for you. From *The American Heritage Dictionary*: "implies consciousness of one's own powers and abilities"; and from the *World Book Dictionary* and *Webster's New World Dictionary,* a firm belief in oneself and one's abilities.

Regardless of how capable a woman may be or of how high her level of self-confidence may be, having a handicapped child tends to threaten her belief in herself and in her abilities. Assaults upon her self-confidence begin at the very beginning of her realization that this child is deficient in ability and continue with each incident of his nonachievement until she often feels she is incapable of doing anything successfully. This pattern of defeatism may grow until her self-confidence is so completely shaken she becomes unable to cope with even the minor demands of her role, unless someone steps in to help her raise her assessment of herself. It is your responsibility to help your wife.

A person's self-confidence must be created from within, but appraisal of one's ability is also dependent upon the self-esteem reflected by others. Your wife should not rely heavily upon your words of praise of her, of course, and yet this is a vital ingredient of any successful marriage and absolutely necessary in a marriage when a child is handicapped.

You help your wife develop and maintain her self-confidence in many ways — when you praise her for her accomplishments such as her cooking, her household management ability, her talent in home decorating, et cetera, anything you know she takes pride in doing. Cover-all statements of praise also help her improve her opinion of herself (as well as letting her know you appreciate her ability) .

"Honey, you are amazing. How do you manage to do all that you do and do it so well?"

"You are such a good wife."

"How do you manage to have so much patience with Johnny? He would never have made so much progress if you hadn't helped him so much."

Or, "I'm glad you spoke up at the meeting tonight. You always speak well, and you expressed just what everyone else was thinking."

Supportive statements such as these help a woman develop her self-confidence as much as anything else and lay the groundwork for, "Of course, you can do it," when the "it" may be anything from upholstering a chair, to giving a party, to teaching and training your child; or if and when the time should come, to being strong enough to let your child live in a residential school.

Hand in hand with being aware of your wife's need for your words of praise and encouragement is the need for you to temper your criticism of her. Little else can so effectively weaken a wife's self-confidence as having to listen to a constant barrage of criticism from her husband. In any type of close relationship between two people, there are times when disapproval must be expressed, of course. Criticism in any form is always potentially dangerous to a relationship, but there are constructive rather than destructive ways of expressing disapproval. Be gentle and sparing with your criticism; consider your wife's feelings and the problems she faces.

Another effective way of boosting your wife's sense of her own capability is by encouraging her to use and develop her abilities and talents that are not concerned with her roles of wife and mother. Helping her to expand the horizons of her accomplishments may mean encouraging her to work at a job outside the home, or supporting her efforts to develop some talent such as painting, music, needlework, et cetera, or to become involved with school, church, or community activities. The satisfaction of successful accomplishment of projects will strengthen her self-confidence and help her be a better mother and wife.

Lifting Your Wife's Moods of Depression   Depression is one of the most common "ailments" afflicting mothers of handicapped children and can range from temporary moods of "the blues" to prolonged serious emotional instability. The serious depression of emotional instability has roots that lie far back in previous experiences and requires the help of a professional counselor. The "blue" or "low spirit" moods are temporary dejection usually caused by a feeling of being overwhelmed by the problems of everyday life, although frequently no direct problem can be isolated as being the direct cause. It is this type of depression which you can help your wife overcome.

A mother who has a handicapped child frequently experiences depression for many good and logical reasons. She is constantly under the pressure of extraordinary responsibility for this child in so many areas of his learning and dependence and often feels she carries the weight of a tremendous burden from which there is no relief or escape. Another frequent cause is frustration, because she sees so little evidence that what she does for her child helps him progress. In addition there are myriad other causes, such as a feeling of futility and failure and lack of purpose in her life.

You can do much to alleviate and lessen the causes of your wife's depression. Your words of praise and encouragement will help convince her that she is capable of coping with her problems, and your reassurance of your love for her strengthens her sense of worth. But, often you will need to take more definite, simple constructive measures.

For instance, since just pure and simple overwork often contributes to a mother's depression, finding some way to lighten her workload will ease many of the pressures. If the cost of household help can possibly be fitted into your budget, it may well be worth giving up something which is not absolutely necessary — just weekly or occasional help with housecleaning may be all that is needed. Or, if household help is out of the question, *you* can help with housekeeping chores, especially the heavier tasks such as mopping the floors or helping with the laundry. Take notice of all that your wife must do and remember that she is not a superwoman — she cannot do everything. The term "harried housewife" is no joke; it is reality, especially when a child is handicapped.

Boredom is another frequent contributor to depression. Even though a mother's day is completely filled (and often overfilled) with her duties, she can be bored because of the dullness of repetition. Sometimes an attack of boredom-blues can be cured by a change of scenery — an evening out, having company, going on a picnic or for a drive. You might offer to baby-sit so your wife can be free to go shopping or visiting or to do whatever she wants to do by herself. Mothers often feel they can spare neither the time nor the money for something just for themselves, so encourage your wife (or support her own efforts) to find some hobby or activity which will be interesting and challenging for her.

Holding a job outside the home can be a very effective method of relieving depression. Being able to contribute to the family finances gives many women a feeling of usefulness, and a job can also provide a woman with challenge and a sense of purpose which she may be denied because her child's handicap limits the scope of her motherhood. A word of caution, though: a job is not the answer for every woman. If your wife feels that her responsibility to her family prohibits her going out to work, do respect her desire not to work outside her home.

Poor physical condition can also cause depression. There are many reasons why mothers, and especially mothers of handicapped children, tend to overlook their own medical needs. Caring for their children leaves little time for themselves; medical expenses are already high because of their children's needs; often it is difficult to find someone to look after a handicapped child so his mother can keep an appointment with a doctor. Your wife's health is your concern and part of your responsibility toward her. Impress upon her the importance of being healthy — you need her, your child needs her, and you are concerned for her because you love her. If necessary, offer to baby-sit so she can keep a doctor's appointment; assure her that medical expenses for her are as necessary as for your child.

Help Your Wife Expand Her Strengths   Your wife has a basic foundation of inner strength of character; now she needs your help in developing and expanding that strength. Because each marriage relationship and each family situation is unique, no hard and fast guidelines can be given, but certain attitudes will apply to every couple.

Assure your wife that you will be there to support her and to understand if she should falter in her attempts to solve the problems that face her as she strives to be a good wife and mother. Accept that she *is* trying. Encourage her by letting her know you believe she is capable of coping with the now altered pattern of her life.

Support your wife as she makes the effort to reach outside her previous range of proven successful achievements to try new endeavors, including even the practical challenges of her everyday life. Strength of will and of resolve develop slowly and step by step as challenges are met and goals are successfully achieved. Your wife needs the strength that your reassurance of her capability and your respect for her determination to try gives to her.

Because of what happened to your child, you now both find yourselves suddenly faced with the necessity of reaching instant maturity (or so it probably seems to you). Now there seems to be no time for the usual trial-and-error learning from experiences, of the slow but sure growth from one stage of responsibility to the next. Both of you must find resources of strength of character and determination that far exceed what would be expected of you were your child not handicapped.

The key word is *both* — it is not expected, not even healthy, that one of you should carry the burden of responsibility for your child alone. To be successful, both of you must strive to expand your own strengths and help each other realize and develop that basic strength each possesses. There must be a melding of personalities, a dovetailing of the strong personality traits of one with those of the other. Through this "dovetailing" or blending, the union of your two separate personalities is fused into one strong unit, whereby neither loses his identity and each is helped by the other in developing strength and expanding capability.

That Demon, Money Unless you are among the very few families fortunate enough to have a high income, finances are going to be a problem for you. Although insurance coverage, community help and resources, and taxation have greatly improved in recent years for families who have handicapped children, much of the extra expense of treatment and care still must be borne by the parents — and this extra expense strains the financial resources of any family.

Because of this ever-present burden, you can expect that you and your wife will have disagreements about spending. The only really effective way to keep these disagreements down to a minimum is through open, honest discussion so that misunderstandings can be cleared up and problems solved together. Lay your financial cards on the table and be honest with each other about bills, purchase of major needs and minor wants, household expenses, et cetera. Learn how to talk together without accusations that will hurt each other's feelings. It is very important, too, that you keep your wife informed about your financial condition — your income (you'd be surprised how many wives don't know how much their husbands earn), your savings, debts, retirement income, even the fact that the family car needs a major tune-up or that the roof needs to be replaced. Don't justify your secrecy by believing you are protecting her, wives seldom need this kind of protection. Now, don't go overboard, either, and add to her own worries by constantly airing your own financial problems to her.

Remember, to develop a successful marriage husband and

wife must work together, and this applies to money matters just as much as it is applicable to any other facet of their marriage relationship.

Marriages Do Sometimes Fail   Not every married couple is able to withstand the pressures and strains placed on their relationship by having a child who is handicapped. One or the other, or both, fails to meet the needs of the other.

There are many reasons for failure, of course, but the underlying cause is seldom the child and his handicap, nor can the fault often be placed on one parent. Just as it takes the efforts of both husband and wife to make a marriage succeed, so does it take both to break a marriage apart. When the differences between them cannot be overcome although *both have earnestly tried,* then it may be best for all concerned that the marriage be dissolved. If you should find yourself in this situation, don't blame your child — the problems between you and your wife were present before he was and before you knew about his handicap.

Summary   Having a child who is handicapped is one of the most traumatic circumstances which can happen to a marriage. Even if the handicap is one which can be corrected (such as cleft palate) or can be overcome eventually (such as some learning disorders), the depth and range of the problems are enormous. Because this child is a part of each and a further extension of themselves, the parents' emotional reactions are intense, feelings are unusually sensitive, and otherwise unimportant facets of their personalities tend to become overemphasized.

No two people react in exactly the same manner to any given set of circumstances and certainly not to the catastrophe of a child's handicap, but because of the similarity of human feelings, the need of each parent for the other one is always increased and broadened by what happened to their child. Only by recognizing, responding to, and accepting this need for each other can they then become strong enough to cope independently with adjustment.

There is no magical formula, no secret cure-all, but if there were it would be something like this — develop your ability to think first of your wife and of her need of you before thinking of yourself. Isn't that what love is really all about? In any marriage both must respond to the needs of the other one. Having a handicapped child intensifies the responsibility each must assume for the other one, but this reciprocal need is not the childish "I can't live without you," but rather "With you beside me to encourage me and support me, I can develop my own inner strength. I am able to do it alone if I had to do so, but it is easier if you are with me."

7. Especially for Fathers

It is generally assumed that it is the mother for whom adjustment is the greater problem, and so major concern is usually for her. But the realization of his child's being handicapped is also traumatic for a father, and his life is also changed, for whatever plans he makes for himself and for his family must be made in consideration of his child's extraordinary dependency upon him.

Although many aspects of adjustment are similar for both mother and father because these concern parenthood, some phases are unique to a father's role because his areas of parent-responsibility are different from a mother's. Since providing for his family's financial needs is predominantly the father's responsibility, this will be the aspect of adjustment that will affect you most. There will be many times when you will feel depressed by the burden of your financial responsibility; times, perhaps, when you will resent the need for security that deprives you of your freedom of choice in your working life. You will wonder, too, whether your child is worth all the worry, the strain, and the material assets you must deny yourself and the rest of your family because of the cost of his needs.

Adjusting your dreams and ambitions for your child will not be so hard, once you realize through your own good common sense that no parent can determine his child's goals of accomplishment; he can only guide him in developing his capabilities. Since you are human, you will suffer pangs of disappointment at times because your child's lack of ability deprives you of pride in his accomplishments, but if you will teach yourself to see the good qualities he has and not to concentrate on what he does not have, you will find your disappointment lessened. And, just as you did when you were trying to learn to accept the reality of his handicap, you must exert an effort to learn what his limits of ability are. Go to see the doctor with your wife and talk to him yourself, rather than relying upon her to give you the information. Read about your child's handicap, talk to others you may know who have handicapped children, gather information from many sources.

Sometimes you will want to cry out, "Hey, look at me! I'm having problems, too, and I need help." But you don't because you feel sure there is no one to hear or to help. But don't despair, there are people to whom you can turn for help and understanding; there are solutions to your problems, and you will find ways to manage.

One valuable source for help and understanding is other parents of handicapped children. Attending parents' group meetings is one of the best ways to find this source of help. There you can talk to parents — especially to fathers — whose children are also handicapped, and what you learn from their experiences will help you help yourself. You may even find a sense of relief just from being able to share your worries and fears with those you know understand how you feel because they have had the same experience.

You will survive; you will manage to cope with the burdens of your responsibility. You will rise above this adversity, because you have many sources of inner strength you will learn to use. When you realize that you cannot let yourself look upon your child's handicap as *your* handicap, you will learn that life can be rich and fatherhood rewarding.

Exercise Your Rights as Father

Your child will have many needs that only you can fulfill, but the greatest of these needs is your love. And, you will find that much of your pain and disappointment will be eased when you feel free to express your love to him. Taking care of a child, meeting his needs, is a parent's responsibility; loving his child is a parent's right. Do not hesitate or be afraid to exercise that right.

All children welcome the attention they receive from their fathers. Mother is usually around all the time, but father's time is something extra-special, so you'll find the door already open, and your child already in a receptive frame of mind for your attention. Since child care is predominantly a mother's responsibility, it is natural that your wife spends much more time with your child than you are free to do, but there are still many opportunities you can find to fulfill his need of knowing your love and attention. Even the most severely mentally retarded child responds to love and affection — and needs love and affection desperately. Spending time with your child, playing with him, and teaching him is loving him.

You can hold and cuddle him as you would any child, but much of what you do with your son or daughter will have to be altered to fit the handicapping lack of ability. Consider, for example, playing. Play has many values for parent and child — it is fun, both get to know each other, and it is a valuable learning tool for the child. Perhaps you cannot play football with your physically handicapped son, but there are other play activities he can participate in that you both will enjoy. Teaching your blind or visually handicapped child to use building blocks will demand great patience, but his success will give you a feeling of pride that will help to offset your disappointment that he is not like other children. Reading aloud must be adapted for a mentally retarded child's understanding, but his enjoyment and pleasure will open new avenues of love for both of you. Methods of communicating with deaf children have been developed, and it is necessary that a child with such a handicap learn how to adapt himself to a hearing world while he is within the safety of his family circle — what better

way than by playing with his father? Learn to adapt your playing activities to your child's abilities and mental age, rather
than to what you would expect from his chronological age.
Learn, too, to accept the small achievements he accomplishes
as being milestones of progress in his development. Above all,
enjoy your child; revel in the pleasure his love of you and his
affection give to you.

Physical therapy is prescribed as treatment for the majority
of handicapping deficiencies. Since the exercises are usually
performed daily on a definite schedule, by taking charge of
one of your child's daily sessions, you will be helping him learn
and develop as you also let him know he is important to you.
By learning more about his disabilities, you will be encouraged
by the progress you will see him making. Knowing that you
are helping him make this progress will give you a feeling of
pride and satisfaction.

Tasks usually considered chores of child care can also be
pleasure times for you and for your child; bathtime, for example, can be fun. Splashing, the relaxing effect of the warm
water, and laughing are happy sources of togetherness. (This
is particularly important when the child is older and heavier,
and especially if the child is a boy.)

Even if your child is severely handicapped, he will enjoy
many of the same fun activities that other children enjoy. He,
too, likes trips to the park where he can swing on the swings
and ride the merry-go-round. As he grows older, he will enjoy
other activities like eating out, going to ball games or to the
movies. So, you need not be deprived of your child's companionship because he is handicapped; just adapt to his abilities.

Financial Responsibility

These suggestions are for the everyday situations of family
living, but there are ways of coping with your most important

responsibility to your child — your financial responsibility for his extra medical care, therapy, training, and future welfare.

It is the future that often looms most menacingly over a father's thoughts and plans. His child's welfare is a great responsibility, but there are ways of easing the weight of this burden if plans are begun during the earlier years. There are special types of insurance benefits that can be adapted for providing for a handicapped child (remember, you are not the first father, nor are you alone, to need special plans for your child. The major insurance companies have handled such situations as yours before and are experienced in knowing how to advise you). At the present time (1973), the Social Security Act ruling is that a child who became dependent before he reached age twenty-one is eligible for benefits at the time his father reaches the age of eligibility or in the event of the father's death or disability. Unfortunately, that leaves a large span of years when the cost of a child's care must be borne by his father. But there are other sources of help, such as the various state and federal child welfare agencies, the organizations dedicated to helping children and their families who suffer the same handicap your child has. Large national service organizations, such as Lions International, Shriners, and many others also are sources of financial help.

But most of the responsibility will have to be met by you, and if you are like most men in your circumstances, you are concerned with how to keep this situation of your child's being handicapped from being a hindrance to you in your career. Of course, it will be harder for you, but having the responsibility of a handicapped child does not necessarily mean you will be unable to achieve success in your own life. I have known many men who have risen to great heights of success, despite being "burdened" with a handicapped child. Perhaps they were spurred on to greater achievement by determination to overcome their disappointment, surely by the need to establish a more secure future for their children. But, it really makes no difference what the driving force was behind their accomplishments, and no doubt if any were asked, they could not say. They did succeed in making something useful of their lives by exerting that extra measure of determination — regardless of being dealt a blow that could easily have defeated them, they did not succumb to defeat.

Now, with all this discussion about succeeding, there is also a caution. Do not let your professional life or your desire to succeed overshadow your family's need for you. Remember, you are a father and a husband, too, and this part of your life is as important as your responsibility to your career. Just as any father must do, you have to strive to reach a balance between your work life and your family life. You cannot afford to deprive your family of the benefit of your attention and proof of your love.

I asked one father — an outstanding example of success in his particular field — how he had managed to accomplish all that he had and still spend enough time with his family to establish a warm relationship with his children. "I fought with that problem for a long time," he said, "and then an older and wiser man than I told me that if I were careful about the quality of the time I spent with my family, the quantity would not be so important; that because I had so little time to spend at home, I had to make darn sure I was giving my undivided attention to my family whenever I was around."

So there is your answer — it is the *quality* of the time you spend with your family, not so much the *quantity*.

I believe that even more so than mothers, fathers are haunted by the question "Why me? Why did this happen to *me?*" The best answer I can give you is the answer another father of a handicapped child gave himself. "Why *not* me?" The father's only son's excellent mind is trapped inside a body so severely handicapped by cerebral palsy that he is unable to communicate orally and even using a typewriter is extremely difficult. This man built his small one-man operation into a company large enough to employ several hundred. He and his wife have been active in church and civic activities, and theirs is a happy household, full of the joy of living and giving and of love. Their other child, a daughter two years younger than their son, recently returned from a two-year stint as a Peace Corps worker and will soon receive her teacher's certificate in special education. Their son has received every benefit of treatment, therapy, and training they could find for him in clinics, special classes, and residential schools. He lives at home now, and they refuse to let him hide — or to hide from society themselves. With a motorized wheelchair and a special ramp for easier entrance into the stationwagon-van, he is able to accompany them on many excursions. Some day he will have to return to the residential school he visits for several weeks about twice a year, but for the present, this family enjoys life, inspiring others while they are doing so.

For other men, having a handicapped child has another kind of effect on their careers. Often what a man learns about himself and about others becomes a turning point in his life toward greater achievement. One of the leading orthopedic surgeons in this part of the country decided to specialize in this branch of medicine after his daughter was diagnosed as being cerebral palsied. I know a psychiatrist who added extra years to his training so that he could help other children who also suffer from mental illness similar to his child's. A chemist whose research has helped provide a vital missing link to understanding some of the causes of mental retardation has mentally retarded twin sons. A young technician, while working as a pattern die-maker, designed a device for relieving the accumulation of fluids around the brain (hydrocephalus) that was damaging his son. The world is full of men who have refused to let their lives be ruined and have found great rewards in self-satisfaction and achievement by turning their talents toward helping others, fulfilling a need for society that they would never have been aware of had they not had a handicapped child.

Your adjustment will be successful only if you learn to look at the past as being done and over with and place your concern with today's goals to be achieved. Live each day for itself — without backward looks or deciding what goals of accomplishment you will expect your child to achieve tomorrow. Do not just "live each day as if it were your last," but *enjoy* each day for that special gift it is. Love your child and enjoy him for the special person he is. Accept this catastrophe not as a tragedy, but as a challenge; be determined to rise above this adversity and become the person you are capable of being.

8. Especially Concerning Siblings

WHEN A CHILD is handicapped, every member of his family is affected. In many ways his nonhandicapped siblings (brothers and sisters) are affected more than his parents, because the whole development of a child's personality is influenced by having a brother or sister who is handicapped. Because of the crisis this creates for the family, any nonhandicapped child will face many stressful incidents of acute difficulty. If there are older children, the advent of a handicapped child into the family causes a definite turning point in their lives, a change far more traumatic and abrupt than simply the addition of another child. If the handicapped child is the oldest, any other children enter a family whose life pattern has already been made different.

Whether the influence of having a handicapped sibling is to be detrimental to a child's developing personality, or whether he will be able to cope with the problems this will inevitably cause him, depends upon the parents. If their attitude is one of calm acceptance of their handicapped child and his limited ability, and if they strive to create a home atmosphere full of love and security in which each child is respected as an individual with unique needs and particular capabilities, they will then lay the foundation for good family and sibling adjustment.

The responsibility of raising a handicapped child is certainly great, but no more so than for nonhandicapped siblings. Being a parent under such a situation is difficult, frustrating, and complicated — to say the least — but the rewards can be so very great. To observe the deep compassion for others your child learns to have and the will and determination he develops to make his life worthwhile and meaningful, to know you have taught your child that it is possible to rise above great difficulties and see him then have faith in himself and trust in the future — what greater rewards can a parent have? These are the qualities of character that can be instilled and nourished by parents if they work together to help their nonhandicapped children accept and adjust to having a handicapped sibling.

Sibling Emotional Reaction

A child's life is different when there is a handicapped sibling, and if you are to teach your normal child (or children) how to cope with the many difficult situations he will encounter and give him the right guidance, you must have an insight into his emotional reactions to having a brother or sister who is handicapped.

The result of some studies conducted in this country and in Great Britain show that certain general reactions appear to be consistent with all children who have handicapped siblings. (These parallel what I have also observed from experiences with my own three sons, as well as from other families I've known.) Although siblings do not follow the same patterns and order of emotional reaction as their parents, and the causes and manifestations of their feelings often are different, they do experience the same basic reactions of resentment, hostility, shame, denial, even guilt and grief, as their parents. Children's emotional reactions differ, too, according to age and, to some extent, the severity and type of handicap.

Because he is a child, a sibling's reaction is primarily directed toward himself and how *his* life is affected by his handicapped brother or sister. Consequently, he is influenced more by how he feels his parents treat him as compared with their treatment of his handicapped sibling than he is by the reality of the condition itself.

As you endeavor to apply the insight you will gain from understanding these general sibling reactions, keep one concept in the forefront of your mind — always be honest with your normal child about his brother's or sister's handicap. This is the basic policy which must be strictly adhered to if your efforts to teach and guide him are to be successful. Answer any questions as truthfully as possible, according to his age and level of comprehension. Do not try to hide the limits of your handicapped child's ability from him and be honest about the prospects of his future development and improvement.

Be truthful also with yourself and your observance of your nonhandicapped child's actions. Do not try to ignore signs that warn of trouble out of fear that recognition would indicate your failure as a parent. Do not try to cope with all his problems alone, but be wise enough to seek help from your doctor or a professionally trained child counselor.

The following discussion is intended to serve only as a general guide for helping parents understand how their other children may feel about having a handicapped sibling, and some of the problems that children in similar situations frequently face. Rather than offering "cures," my intention is to make parents aware that any such child needs special consideration, attention, and understanding and to encourage parents to listen to their hearts in respect to all their children.

Resentment   Resentment is perhaps the most consistently overriding reaction children feel toward a handicapped sibling. Now, it is perfectly natural for a child to feel resentment toward brothers and sisters — every child feels at times that his parents do more for another child in the family, that discipline is less severe for another child (especially those who are younger), that another child in the family is given more privileges. This sort of natural, expected resentment, however, usually is only temporary and relates to some particular incident.

There are justifiable causes of sibling resentment, of course. If a child has outstanding talent, he may be given special consideration and receive more than his due share of his parents' attention; the only daughter may be favored over her brothers or the only son over his sisters. Most often, though, the favored child is the child who needs his parents more than do his siblings.

A child's resentment toward his handicapped sibling is seldom temporary, for the situation is permanent. A child who is handicapped has a disproportionate need for his parents' concern and attention; his needs demand a larger share of the family budget than those of his less dependent brothers and sisters; the activities of the family's life must often be planned around what he is capable of doing or his special needs.

The causes of sibling resentment change as time alters needs and situations — the small child resents having less of his mother's attention and time because his handicapped sibling requires so much; the older child resents the restraints placed on his social life or denial of his wants due to the cost of treatment and training necessary for his handicapped sibling's development. It may be that the older child resents having to look after and help a handicapped brother or sister.

How to be fair to all the children? How can parents help them understand and accept all the extras a handicapped child must receive? To such parents life often seems to be a constant juggling act, trying to balance what can be given to each child without denying the other children what they need, too. But isn't that how life is in any family with more than one child? Sacrifice for each other is all part of being a family — the trouble comes when one member (in this instance the nonhandicapped child) is made to sacrifice constantly for another and little or no special consideration is given for his own desires and needs.

The nonhandicapped sibling (or siblings) must be made to feel that he is very special, too. He needs special "treats" —

a day alone now and then with his mother or father, perhaps, or an outing planned particularly for him. Every effort must be made by his parents to arrange for his not being denied the normal activities his friends participate in such as Scouts, sports, or social activities, even if this means foregoing or postponing something that is not absolutely necessary for the handicapped child's needs.

Parents must be careful, also, not to take unfair advantage of their nonhandicapped children in other ways, such as too frequent baby-sitting or entertaining the handicapped child. Little girls, particularly, may enjoy "mothering" their dependent sibling, and this is good for them and for the whole family, but the exaggerated sense of responsibility which they may develop can be harmful to them by denying them the rights of a childhood free from undue responsibility.

Being honest with the nonhandicapped child also helps lessen his resentment. When his parents have explained to him that "Johnny must have these braces so his legs will get stronger and he can walk," he has a tangible reason he can accept for not having a new bicycle.

But caution — although the nonhandicapped child's needs are fewer, he also has a great need for special attention from his parents and for the rights and privileges to which he is entitled.

Jealousy Resentment can quickly grow into jealousy, and it is often very hard to distinguish between the two. To be jealous is to be: "fearful of being supplanted; apprehensive of loss of position or affection." (Resentment is defined as: "indignation or ill will felt as a result of a real or imagined offense.")

If the other child is given too much cause to feel that his parents "favor" his handicapped sibling, then that brother or sister becomes a rival to be feared lest he supplant the nonhandicapped child in their parents' affection.

A child must be made to feel that he is just as important to his parents as any other child in the family, and although admittedly his need of the parents is less obvious, still it *is* just as important. Because of their immaturity, children lack the ability to reason and to understand the need one child may have over another.

Like resentment, jealousy is a part of every family relationship; but, also like resentment, jealousy must be kept to a minimum for a good family atmosphere.

Hostility   Resentment leads to jealousy, and the jealousy a child feels toward his handicapped sibling can lead to feelings and expressions of hostility.

In many ways this is a perfectly natural human feeling. How can a child not have bitter feelings about the person who (he feels) is the cause of so much of his unhappiness, takes so much away from him — his parents' attention and concern, and even at times their love? The normal child must often cope with the pressure of having to achieve, the denial of so much that he wants for himself, perhaps, even the sadness he sees in his parents and their tension-caused irritability.

Children have not learned how to be objective in their reactions, this being an adult character trait. They are very subjective and see everything that happens in the light of how they are affected personally. Similarly, a child cannot understand that the root of his troubles (or what he sees as his troubles) is the handicapping condition his brother or sister suffers. He sees the source of his problems as the child himself. It is Tommy — or Susie — who is causing his problems; therefore, he directs his hostile feelings directly toward his handicapped sibling.

He may express his hostility through actions that hurt his sibling physically or tease and taunt him because of his inabilities or differentness. He may direct his hostile feelings toward his parents through disobedience, impudence, breaking possessions, et cetera.

The hostile child is a hurting child; hurting because he believes he is not loved by his parents and is not important to them.

A child whose hostile actions are dangerous to his handicapped sibling or to others needs the help of a professional counselor, and this should not be postponed after being noticed, because parents are usually too emotionally involved to be able to handle the situation adequately. On the other hand, a child's rare or one-time show of hostility need not frighten his parents, only alert them to finding out the cause. A child must be disciplined, of course, for any hurtful acts he commits against others, but administration of discipline should be accompanied by efforts to learn what the precipitating cause was.

For example: Mr. and Mrs. B. could not understand how their little daughter, Susie, could have scratched and bruised her legs so badly. She was nearly three years old, but because her cerebral palsied condition was so severe, she could not even turn from her back to her stomach — much less sit alone or move about enough to have hurt herself — or move her arms enough to reach her legs. The bruises and scratches increased over the next few days, and the distraught parents began to fear that the mild cold Susie was recovering from wasn't just a cold after all, but something serious. Then the mystery was solved. One day when Mrs. B. was hanging up clothes in Susie's room while she was napping in her crib, suddenly Susie screamed. Mrs. B. looked around the door and saw their six-year-old, Mary, standing by the crib, "That's right — cry! I hate you! Just because you got sick, I couldn't have my birthday party. I wish you'd die!"

Mary ran out of the room, and when Mrs. B. picked up Susie, she saw fresh scratches on her little legs. That night she told her husband about what had happened, and together they examined what they had been saying to Mary. They realized that it was not just the postponed birthday party which had triggered her action, but all too often she had been told to "play outside, you know how noise upsets Susie," or, "You girls play at Kay's house, Susie is taking her nap." Susie's sleep was important, but Mary had needs, too, which were not being met by her parents. She felt pushed away, her place in her parents' affection replaced by this handicapped little sister.

Guilt A child's guilt concerning his handicapped sibling is different in many ways from his parents' feelings of guilt. His is not the responsibility of having borne a defective child or having allowed something to happen that caused the handicapping condition. There are rare instances when an older sibling is actually responsible for having caused an accident that injured a child, and sometimes a child may even believe that something he did when his mother was pregnant or when his sibling was an infant caused the handicapping condition and be tormented with guilt.

But a child's guilt is more often caused by how he feels about his handicapped sibling, or how he feels about his parents because of him. He knows it is "wrong" to dislike his handicapped brother (or sister), to wish him dead or removed from the family, to resent the extra attention their parents pay him. He also feels guilty because of the way he treats him — because he slapped his defenseless brother or yelled at his mentally retarded sister.

While it is necessary that any child be taught to treat his handicapped sibling with understanding and consideration of his limitations and needs, when too much emphasis is placed on his obligations to this sibling, his guilt may only increase. Unless eased, his feelings of guilt may make the normal child reject his handicapped sibling, or he may feel so ashamed of himself and develop such low self-esteem that he retreats from association with his family and friends.

Much of a child's guilt can be eased if his parents are honest with him, explaining the cause of the handicap and the limits of his sibling's ability to perform and comprehend. Explaining and talking to the nonhandicapped child is not enough, however. He must also feel free to ask questions, express his opinions and even to "confess" to his parents how he feels and what he has done that he thinks is wrong without fear of censure or punishment, but expecting and receiving understanding and guidance from his parents.

Grief Don't ever think that a child does not grieve because his brother or sister is handicapped — children are quite capable of some of the finer emotions concerning others. A child may actually grieve even more than his parents — not for what he has lost, but for what his brother or sister will not have. A child can easily identify with his handicapped sibling, and very often he has a better understanding of what he will be denied because of his lack of ability. A nonhandicapped child may also grieve because he is denied the benefits of having a normal sibling, especially when the handicapped child is the only child of another sex in the family, or when there are only two children in the family.

However, it is rare that a child's grief is the intensely felt emotion it may be to his parents. More often a child's grief is a reflection of the emotions he sees in his parents, so being sympathetic and setting a good example is perhaps the best way to help a child overcome his feelings of grief.

Shame and Embarrassment Shame is usually not a major sibling reaction, although it certainly can occur. A child may be ashamed of his handicapped sibling because he relates his inabilities to some family weakness — as with mental retardation, certain other learning difficulties, or hyperactivity. If, however, his parents have resolved their own feelings of shame and show by their actions and words that they are not ashamed of having a handicapped child, their other children will have less cause for shame. Children mimic their parents and assume their feelings and attitudes.

Embarrassment is the greater problem. Being embarrassed about their handicapped brother or sister is perhaps the second most prevalent emotional reaction that nonhandicapped siblings experience. Children usually are more embarrassed than their parents are, especially if the handicapping condition is obvious like severe mental retardation of physical disfigurement. An older child also suffers more painful embarrassment than does a younger child.

Because his family is more important to him than his friends are, the younger child may be quite able to handle the taunts of his friends about his handicapped sibling and feel a sense of loyalty to him and the need to protect him. But embarrassment becomes an acute problem when the nonhandicapped sibling reaches the teen years. Peer approval is so very important during adolescence, and teenagers can be very cruel to each other. Thus, the adolescent may be quite willing to be seen in public with his handicapped sibling when he is far away from home, but absolutely refuse to take him into the grocery store or to the neighborhood movie or bowling alley, or to entertain his own friends at home if there is the slightest danger that his handicapped sibling will be seen by them. This is not because of any lack of his love or consideration, rather he feels inadequate to cope with what his friends may say or think.

The age of the handicapped child also has an effect on his sibling's embarrassment. Usually, the handicapping condition is not so noticeable when the child is younger, and he may be very appealing in his helplessness. Little girls may enjoy "mothering" a young handicapped child, and little boys may accept one into their play when his lack of ability is not yet so very different from theirs or when they can enjoy teaching a less able child.

If parents accept their nonhandicapped child's embarrassment as being reasonable (it is, to him), if they let him know they understand and respect his feelings and do not try to force him to associate in public with his handicapped sibling, then time will often take care of many of the problems.

Of course, a sibling's ability to cope with embarrassment depends upon the example his parents have set before him. If they show by their attitudes that they accept their handicapped child as a full-fledged member of the family, that they are not ashamed of him or embarrassed by his actions, then their non-handicapped children will have a firm foundation of acceptance upon which to build their own acceptance and good adjustment.

Rejection Sibling rejection often closely parallels parental reaction in both cause and manifestation. Resentment, jealousy, guilt, and embarrassment may grow to an overwhelming reaction against which a child cannot fight, so he rejects the very reality of the handicapping condition. The only method he knows of to cope with this distressing situation is to deny that anything is wrong with his brother or sister.

The more frequent reaction, however, is rejection of the handicapped child by refusing to show any affection or to accept any responsibility for his safety or well-being. He may try to shut his handicapped sibling out of his consciousness by ignoring his existence.

And certainly it is the very unusual family in which a normal child does not feel at times that he is being rejected by his parents because of the attention they pay to his handicapped sibling.

Relieving the other reaction problems a nonhandicapped child has also helps to relieve his rejection. If his parents try to be particularly careful to see that he has little or no reason to feel rejected by them and that he is as important to them as is his handicapped sibling, he can then usually accept the reality of his sibling's condition.

Summary In a very capsule and abbreviated discussion, these are the typical reactions a nonhandicapped sibling of a handicapped child may be expected to experience. Because children are so different, and because each family is unique, all children do not experience the same reactions, nor will they react with the same degree of intensity to similar reactions.

Any child can be expected to have some negative feelings about his siblings, even without the extraordinary problems created by a brother's or sister's lack of ability. When, however, a family includes a handicapped child, the negative emotional reactions his siblings experience become more significant, the effect more lasting upon the development of their personalities.

This effect certainly doesn't have to be detrimental, and if the parents are aware of how a normal child may be affected by having a handicapped sibling, then they are better equipped to understand the problems he faces and to handle their responsibility to him more effectively.

Do not let the responsibility of being an effective parent to your nonhandicapped child frighten you, and don't let the stumbling blocks you will surely trip over upset you. Be patient — with yourself as well as with your child — and keep your eye focused on the distant goal of the happy, well-adjusted adult you are helping him become. Relax and enjoy him, and let him know you do. He does have unique problems, but then so does *every* child.

The Special Needs of Nonhandicapped Siblings

Because of the overwhelming concern for the handicapped child in the family and the great amount of time and money which must often be spent to meet his needs, parents frequently find that they have little attention left for their other children. But when the family includes a handicapped child, his siblings need special consideration and understanding from their parents, too. Since under these circumstances life can never be normal for these children, they are presented with many problems they would ordinarily not have to face. In many ways they are in the same boat of confusion as parents often find themselves, except that a child has the added disadvantage of youth and inexperience. In some respects they may also be considered "handicapped," because like their physically or mentally disabled siblings, they are unable to cope with the unusual problems of their life without help.

So, if the effect of having a handicapped sibling is not to be harmful to the nonhandicapped child's developing personality, his parents must also be cognizant of *his* special needs and help *him* with his unique problems.

The Need for Honesty   The necessity for parents to be honest and truthful with their other children about their handicapped child has been mentioned before, and because this is so important, it will be mentioned again in the following discussion. Unless a policy of complete honesty is strictly adhered to, parents cannot hope to build an effective relationship with their nonhandicapped children.

Some sixth sense told me this was true, and this is the principle we have tried to follow with our own three sons. Working with families of handicapped children over the years, my observations seemed to prove my theory correct. Then, when I asked several siblings of handicapped children what would be the most important advice they thought parents should be told, their unanimous agreement was "to be honest. Tell the other children the true facts — what caused the handicap, just how disabled the child really is, why he needs all the special treatment and training, what improvement can be hoped for in the future." The older siblings said, "Tell them to be honest, too, about plans for the child's future — what arrangements have been made for his care and who is expected to look after him."

"I wouldn't go out for any kind of sports when I was young, because I was scared I'd be hurt like Charley had been and that I'd be mentally retarded, too."

"I used to wake up every morning scared to move my legs, because I was afraid that whatever had happened to make

George cerebral palsied might have happened to me while I was asleep."

One of the young adults said, "I wouldn't date when I was in high school, not even for class parties, because I was afraid I'd fall in love and want to get married, and if I had any children they'd be like my sister."

"If my parents had only explained that Johnny was so bad because he couldn't control his actions, I think I could have been much more patient with him — and with my parents for letting him get away without punishment when I'd be punished for doing the same thing."

But one young man, after being told what the others had replied, said, "I can see I'm really lucky. My parents always told me the truth. I always knew my brother was mentally retarded and that a birth injury had been the cause. I can remember being really mad sometimes when my folks couldn't afford to buy something I wanted because Timmy's special school tuition or medical bills or therapy had to be paid for — but deep down, I also knew that this was more important than whatever it was that I wanted. They never harped about what sacrifices we should make for him, but they sure made no bones about explaining to my sister and me that all they could do was to do the best they could for each of us and to try to give to each what was most important. I feel responsible for Timmy, in a way, if something should happen to my parents, but I know they made arrangements for him long ago. I don't really understand how my parents did it, but somehow they managed to teach us that Timmy was very special — but then, my sister and I always have thought that we were very special to our parents, too."

A Sibling's Need for Security   Security is one of the basic needs of all children. If a child is to mature into a self-confident adult, his growing-up years must be reasonably "free from fear, doubt, and anxiety." Material wealth is not so very important so long as the basic needs are satisfied; the criterion is how rich the family is in love, for security to a child means being confident that his parents love him and that he is important to them.

Regardless of his parents' attitudes and the quality of family unity, the presence of a handicapped child in the family always represents a threat to the other children's sense of security. The more understanding and the more consideration parents show their nonhandicapped children, the less they feel threatened, but the danger of insecurity is still present. A child who has a handicapped sibling has many reasons for being anxious about his parents' love of him, much reason to doubt that they consider him important, and many instances that arouse the fear that his more dependent brother or sister will replace him in his parents' affection.

Sibling Rights and Privileges If the parent-child relationship is to insure and protect the child's sense of security, his rights as an individual must be respected, and he must be assured of being granted the basic privileges he is due as an equally important member of the family.

Parental recognition of a child as a separate identity includes making an effort to know and understand his reactions to having a handicapped sibling. Respecting his reactions and trying to help him cope with his problems assures him that he is an important member of his family. He must also be given the freedom and opportunity to develop his abilities — within the limits of his capability.

I think one of the most difficult aspects of trying to be a good parent to one's normal children is controlling the very natural desire to expect too much of them and to push them into accomplishments that will serve to compensate for the handicapped child's lack of ability. Especially when the handicapped child is the eldest, it is hard to adjust one's standards of mature reasoning and behavior to a logical level for the other children.

These children's rights and privileges must be protected by

the parents in other ways too. Family life should not be allowed to revolve completely around the handicapped child and his needs. This attitude is unhealthy for the parents and the child himself and grossly unfair to the other children. Of course, the handicapped child's needs must often be placed ahead of the others', but too much emphasis on meeting his needs forms fertile ground for the development of resentment.

Consider the seemingly minor question of vacation and leisure activities. Naturally, these will be somewhat determined by the needs and abilities of the handicapped child, but all such activities should not revolve around him. Some way to adjust them to the other children's desires must be found, even if this means leaving the handicapped child with willing relatives or a paid baby sitter occasionally.

(In many parts of the country, camps for handicapped children are conducted by various organizations such as chapters of United Cerebral Palsy and local service clubs. Such camps offer valuable training and experiences for these children and also provide parents with an opportunity to participate in activities with their other children which would not be possible if the handicapped child had to be included.)

One of the most difficult kinds of decisions parents of handicapped children must make is whether to follow a suggested treatment or therapy in the *hope* that the child will be helped when the cost of time and/or money would mean denial for their other children. There is no simple answer. All that parents can do is question the doctors and try to ascertain how much of an effect this will have on his development, how necessary it really is. Then they must weigh carefully all they have learned and consider which child's need is the most important.

Julie and Bob faced just such a decision. Their daughter, Karen, is cerebral palsied, but her only handicap is physical — involving her legs — and her learning ability is above average. When Karen was about eight years old, the orthopedist recommended surgery that might enable her to walk. The cost of the surgery would mean that four-year-old Charley would have to drop out of nursery school, and there would be no way to afford some rather extensive orthodontic work fourteen-year-old Catherine needed to straighten her teeth, and she would also have to discontinue her dancing lessons. After much thought, consultation, and discussion with the doctor, Julie and Bob decided that the possible benefit for Karen was more important for her development than what the other children would be denied. They called a family conference and told the children of their decision, explaining the particulars to them. Although the surgery was not successful, the family felt closer because they understood why the parents had made the decision and because they had all participated in the effort to help Karen.

Carolyn and Mike's decision was similar, but the circumstances were different. Their oldest child, Stephen, is cerebral palsied, too, but more severely involved than Karen, for he is also mentally retarded and can walk only with the aid of braces. He was twelve when his physical therapist told them about a new concept of therapy that was proving to be successful with children handicapped as Stephen was. At first Carolyn and Mike were tremendously excited at the thought of how Stephen might benefit from this program, but when they learned more about all that was involved — how expensive it would be, how much time both would have to spend with Stephen each day, and how unpredictable the results could be — they began to hesitate. Seven-year-old Mary was having problems in school, and the teacher had suggested that they consult a psychologist about her learning difficulties and perhaps have her take a series of tests. Since there was no school psychologist, this would all have to be done at their expense. They took Mary to a psychologist; a battery of tests revealed that she had perceptual difficulties that could be corrected through special training to improve her motor and visual perception, and her learning problems could be overcome. This therapy was fairly expensive and would also require at least an hour a day of parent-directed home exercises. Carolyn and Mike knew they could not afford both therapy programs, and after much thought and soul-searching, decided to forego the suggested therapy for Stephen in favor of Mary's needs.

Many times, too, a nonhandicapped sibling's needs must be placed ahead of a handicapped child's needs for reasons that are not quite so obvious. A girl may need the self-assurance and social acceptability that dancing class would give her; playing on a neighborhood baseball or football team or participating in other sports is often almost necessary to help a boy with his development and his social adjustment. A new bicycle, rather than a used one, may help the shy child feel more secure among his or her friends.

Similar decisions must be made by all parents, but to parents who have a handicapped child, these decisions often seem harder to make and more significant because so much may depend upon what they decide.

Summary Being a good parent to your nonhandicapped children isn't really so very hard, once you learn to relax and enjoy them and let your natural love for them guide your decisions. You will make mistakes, you will make wrong decisions — you are only human — but seldom will your mistakes have a lasting effect on your children. Having a handicapped child will not harm your effectiveness as a good parent to your nonhandicapped children. Rather, you can be enriched and become a better parent because of what you will have to learn. Rather than being a force to tear your family apart, having a child who is handicapped can be instrumental in helping the parents develop unity and strength among their children. Likewise, a nonhandicapped child can become a stronger, more capable person because of the effect on his life of having a handicapped sibling.

9. Planning for the Future

THE PLANS YOU MAKE for your handicapped child's future will be governed by many factors unique to your particular situation. Among these factors will be the type of handicap your child has, the extent of his disability, and the level of independence that can reasonably be expected of him as an adult. Much of your planning will depend upon the resources that are available in your community for treatment and training, for job opportunities, and perhaps for housing facilities. His need for medical supervision and the availability of such services must also be considered. The opportunities for companionship with others whose level of ability is comparable with his are important factors to be considered, for handicapped children need friends, and social adjustment is as important for a handicapped child as for a nonhandicapped child.

The make-up of the family unit is a very important factor in planning for such a child's future — the presence and needs of other children, whether or not both parents are in the home, the family's financial situation, the mother's health and physical strength, and even the kind of work the father does and the life-style his job demands. The availability of competent household or nursing/child care help and the family's ability to meet this expense may be critical factors.

Since much of the planning for a handicapped child's future is determined by what his needs will be, parents must have some idea of how far he can be expected to develop — whether he can overcome his handicap and eventually be self-supporting, whether he will be semidependent, or whether he will be totally dependent upon others for supplying his basic needs. For these reasons, the parents must be in close communication with the doctors, teachers, and therapists who work with their child and be guided by their opinions and evaluations.

If any planning is to be effective and best for the child and his family, both parents must be in accord. Planning for his future is a two-parent responsibility; in little else in a child's life is parental agreement so important, few other shared responsibilities so great. This is true even if the father is no longer a member of the family unit, so long as he contributes any financial support at all to the child and has any interest in him and concern for his welfare.

The plans parents make for a child who is physically handicapped but whose mental ability is unimpaired will be very different from the plans parents will make for one who is mentally retarded. Because a child whose handicap is physical will be better able to cope with the demands and responsibilities of society as an adult, planning for him is directed toward preparing him for his adult life by providing opportunities for developing his talents and abilities, by encouraging him to reach toward goal-achievement, and inspiring him to have the courage he needs to overcome or to compensate for his disability.

Now, certainly parents should give a mentally retarded child every opportunity available to them for developing his ability and expanding his potential, for he also will need to know the satisfaction of achievement and the fulfillment of contributing to his society. But parents of such a child should direct their planning for the future toward finding an environment into which he will fit and which will meet his particular needs as an adult.

Making plans for a handicapped child's possible future financial dependency should begin as early in his life as possible. Now, most parents of young handicapped children are beset from every side with financial demands that often exceed their ability to meet. Many times the debts incurred for medical treatment, special schooling, therapy, et cetera, take years to repay and making any plans for future financial security seems to be completely out of the question. Still, parents must be aware of the need for *planning* for possible financial obligations for their child. If resources are built up slowly, if special arrangements are made in life insurance policies, retirement benefits, and later, perhaps, through investments, the emotional (and certainly the financial) shock will be lessened. Many mothers keep the plan of going to work or resuming a career in the back of their minds while they gradually prepare themselves for this during their at-home years when their child needs them most. There is a definite need for parents to plan for their future financial reserves, for even when a child overcomes his handicap so that he is able to be partially or completely self-supporting, his parents usually feel much more responsible for him than they do for any nonhandicapped children they may have, and many handicapped children are never able to attain complete financial self-sufficiency.

A fear that most parents of handicapped children share is, "Who will look after my child if something should happen to me?" For peace of mind, if for no other reason, they should make some arrangements for the care of their child during the time he is young, as well as for that time when he reaches maturity, especially if it is expected that he will be semi or totally dependent. Perhaps there are family members — grandparents or uncles and aunts — who can and would be willing to assume responsibility for this child. There may be other children in the family who will assume responsibility for him — particularly after he reaches adulthood — when they become self-supporting. Often this is the more satisfactory arrangement, for most siblings do feel some sense of responsibility for a handicapped brother or sister. However, if plans can possibly be made for the child's financial security, the burden of sibling responsibility is greatly lightened and the accompanying stress lessened. (Be careful with any other children you may have —

don't expect too much of them, and don't overdo efforts to develop their sense of responsibility for this handicapped sibling. Set an example of love and respect for him to guide your other children, so each one will be influenced by "want to" rather than "have to."

Another solution for the care of a handicapped child is permanent residency in a boarding facility. Often for the totally dependent child this is best, especially for those who are mentally retarded. Although those facilities that offer complete care are the most numerous and include state homes or schools, today more attention is being paid to serving the needs of semidependent people through facilities for group living that provide an environment suited to their individual needs and levels of independence without being completely isolated from the community. (See "Residential School is Not Always the Best Solution" near the end of this chapter for more discussion and sources of information about this type of facility).

Although the plans you make are extremely important, no plan must be considered as being absolutely final. Children change as they grow older, and their needs alter. Family situations also change. If present plans don't seem to be best for your child, do not hesitate to make other arrangements. However, you will become frustrated and your child confused if the pattern of his daily life is changed too frequently.

Parents whose children are physically handicapped but have average or above intelligence, may find useful information in the following discussion, but because planning for a mentally retarded child's future is so much more complex in many aspects, the remainder of this chapter is directed primarily toward helping parents whose children are mentally retarded.

Much may not be applicable to parents whose children are "slow learners," for such children are not mentally retarded. A child who is a slow learner is capable of achieving a moderate degree of academic success in the normal classroom, although he may need extra help, and as an adult he will be quite capable of being self-supporting, independent, and socially adjusted. His parents' plans for the future concern helping him develop his talents and abilities so he will be able to adjust to the needs of society. (For example, teaching him that working with his hands is as useful and dignified an occupation as is a professional career, and then providing him with opportunities to develop these skills.)

Making plans for your handicapped child's future may seem to be an awesome responsibility, and at times you may seriously doubt your ability and qualifications to make the right decisions — but do not be dismayed. Keep in mind that your objective is to plan a way of life for him that is appropriate to his individual needs. By letting this principle guide your thoughts, you *will* make the right decisions. Have confidence in yourself and listen to your heart. No one is more capable than you, your child's parents, to make plans that are best for him.

Home versus a Residential Facility

Because of the benefits of concentrated and specialized education and therapy, many physically handicapped children would profit by being in a residential school at some time during their childhood years. Residency would be temporary then, for the purpose of helping the child develop so that he will be able to be an active participant in society and a contributor to his community. When, however, a child is handicapped by a lack of reasoning and learning ability, there may be no place for him in the community, and being unable to adapt to the general society of which he is a part, he would be happier in a life that is adapted to his needs and abilities. Therefore, permanent residency in a boarding school is a decision most often faced by those parents whose children are mentally retarded. For these parents, planning for their child's future nearly always involves deciding whether to keep him at home with the family, or whether it is best for him to live in a residential facility with others whose mental ability is comparable to his.

This is an extremely difficult decision for most parents to make, and I sincerely believe that few other decisions parents of mentally retarded children must make demand more courage and more self-confidence. Whatever their decision, most parents still have some doubt that they have chosen the best life plan for their child. (Also, regardless of their decision, there will always be people who will feel that what they are doing is wrong — and some will not hesitate to voice their criticisms.)

A residential school environment is not best for every child who is mentally retarded, nor is living at home with the family always best. For parents struggling to make this decision, perhaps an outline of certain factors that must be considered will be helpful. For those of you who decide on permanent residency away from home for your child, locating and then selecting the school that best suits your child's needs can be almost as difficult and confusing as making the decision. There are resources available for obtaining information about existing facilities, and certain criteria that those of us who have shared this experience have learned which will be useful to you in selecting the school.

Making the Decision — Home or Residential School?

This is a decision that must be made by the parents. There are many people available to give advice and guidance, but essentially, deciding where a mentally retarded child is to live is a responsibility that must be assumed by his parents.

Now, just as the plans parents make for any handicapped child's future must depend upon professional assessment of his potential abilities and his eventual needs, so must the parents of a mentally retarded child rely upon professional prognosis in deciding where their child should live. When there is a strong possibility that a child will be rather severely mentally retarded, I usually advise his parents to begin thinking about the possibility of eventually placing him in a residential school. The time for making a definite decision does not come, usually, until a child is older, but if parents decide later that a residential school environment will be better for him, the trauma of separation is less if they are already accustomed to the idea, for this then becomes a natural step to be taken in the child's best interest.

So, the first factor parents should consider is the *prognosis for the child's eventual level of development*. This can seldom be definitely determined until a child is older, but a fairly accurate estimation of his ability can be made in most instances — at least near enough to enable them to begin making general plans for his future.

Many different terms are used to classify the mentally retarded according to ability, but those given by Dr. Samuel A. Kirk in his book, *Educating Exceptional Children* (Houghton Mifflin, 1962), seem to me to be the most explanatory. Classification is often made according to a child's IQ, but if you will use Dr. Kirk's terms (or have your child's test results translated into these terms), I believe you will have a clearer understanding of what to expect of your child's particular needs.

(The following explanations are based upon Dr. Kirk's definitions.) An "educable" mentally retarded child will be unable to profit from the regular classroom, but will be able to reach the minimum levels of ability in reading, spelling, and math in a special education program. As an adult he will be able to function independently in the community with guidance and some protection and will be capable of earning a living performing simple tasks. A "trainable" mentally retarded child will be unable to profit from a special education program in the regular school, but is capable of learning the basics of self-care — eating, dressing and undressing, going to the toilet, and sleeping. His social adjustment will be limited to the home and close neighborhood rather than the community. Economically, he will be capable of learning to be useful within the home or a sheltered workshop. A "totally dependent" mentally retarded child is incapable of learning self-care, lacks the ability to be trained for economic usefulness, and will need close supervision throughout his lifetime.

Consequently, another factor to be considered in making the decision as to where a mentally retarded child will live is *the child's need to be protected,* which in turn is based upon his ability to learn and reason — to use what he learns. Where the family lives often determines the extent to which his needs will be met at home. For example, do they live in a small community, where people accept and respect him in the light of his need and his differentness? Or, do they live in an urban neighborhood, where he will not be protected by his neighbors, and where people's acceptance of him is difficult to attain?

The resources available in the community for teaching, training, and therapy the child needs may determine the parents' choice. If special schools and clinics, sheltered workshops, and perhaps group living facilities are available, the benefits of such facilities may far offset the disadvantages of the particular community in which his family lives. Or, if such facilities are not available, perhaps working to establish them would be the parents' best solution.

The child's need for medical care, his general health, and the community resources for meeting this need must also be considered. If, for example, the family lives in an area where specialists and clinics are readily available, often it is best that the mentally retarded child stay at home — at least until the condition of his health has been improved. If, however, they live in a community where medical services are limited or far away, placement in a residential facility where he could receive the medical attention and treatment he needs might be best.

The family situation is a very important factor, as has been mentioned before. This is particularly true when there is only one parent in the family and caring for a mentally retarded child becomes not just difficult, but an actual impossibility. Placement in a residential school may be far better, although the level of his ability is fairly high. Only in rare and unusual circumstances can a mother alone (and it is usually the mother who is in the home in a one-parent situation) find a reliable housekeeper or mother-substitute who can give a mentally retarded child the loving care and the attention he needs.

When there are other children in the family, their needs must also be considered. If the presence of the mentally retarded child in the home means that excessive and unavoidable pressure is placed on family relationships, parents should not blame themselves for not being able to cope with all the various nuances of their responsibilities to all their children. For the sake of their other children's welfare, it might be best that the mentally retarded child live away from home. Also, sometimes a mentally retarded child can feel so threatened and under so much pressure in the natural competition with his nonhandicapped siblings that he cannot help being a disturbance to family harmony.

The mother's health is part of the family situation and should be taken into consideration. Caring for a mentally retarded child is physically demanding and controlling a physically strong mentally retarded child can be an impossible task for one person. Hiring competent help may be impractical, undesirable, or financially impossible for the family. Providing a safe and protected home or yard may also be impossible and may not be best for the child, for isolating him may only serve to further retard his development.

Family income is always a factor that must be considered when trying to plan a dependent child's future living arrangements. Private residential schools can be very expensive, almost like having a child perpetually in college. State schools are usually much less expensive, but are not always desirable for a particular child. So, the benefits a child would receive in a residential school and the benefits to his family must be carefully weighed against the deprivations the rest of the family could possibly suffer.

The cost of keeping a child at home, however, can sometimes be more than the cost of a residential school. One must con-

234 · Adjustment

sider the expense of the necessary therapy and treatment and education; often extra household help is needed; perhaps a second car for needed transportation, or the fact that caring for this child may prevent the mother from holding a job outside the home. All this should be carefully balanced against the expense of a residential school. (Which, by the way, is usually income tax deductible when the main purpose of the facility is for rehabilitation, rather than for custodial care. But, the expenses of therapy, special schools, clinics, and the transportation to and from are also usually deductible when the child lives at home.)

The child's age is another factor — perhaps not so much in deciding if a residential school would be the best environment for him, but rather in deciding when the move should be made. There is no definite rule, for like the other factors, the age a particular child should be placed in a residential school is dependent upon the whole picture of the family situation and the child's needs. "When" is that age when the child will profit more by being in a residential school than he does by being at home. Usually, the best age is sometime between six and twelve years old. By the age of six, family ties are well established; the child knows that he belongs to his family and that he is loved by them. The family, especially other children, will have learned to understand his differentness and needs and to accept him and give him their love. By the time a child is between six and twelve years old, he will have received most of the benefits of parental training through family life as well as through the special schools and clinics. Then, because the parents feel more assured that they have done most of what they can to help him develop, they have less reason to be plagued by guilt that they may be rejecting him and can better evaluate his particular needs.

After the age of twelve, the child may find it hard to make the transition from home to school living. Also, postponing placement may mean that valuable time is lost during which he could be receiving the kind of training that would be most beneficial to his eventual development.

These ages are arbitrary — many children profit more by placement in a residential school at an early age, and many older children (even adults) find in a residential school environment such relief from pressures that their adjustment is quite easy.

The child's size, physical strength, and personality have much to do with his parents' decision. Taking care of a mentally retarded child who is fairly docile and easy to discipline, who has basically a cheerful nature and is not often irritable is quite different from trying to care for a child who cannot be trusted alone for a moment, who is physically strong and uses his strength to rebel against any form of discipline. The one child is obviously happy in the home and brings much happiness to his family; the other is obviously not able to adjust to family life, creating many problems for his parents and disrupting family harmony so much that their natural love of him is overshadowed by their worry and fear for him. Therefore, there may be little reason to place a mentally retarded child who quite obviously is very happy at home with his family in a residential school, regardless of his age. Now, don't think for a minute that parents are always to blame when a child is not happy at home — so much depends upon his basic personality, the level of his learning ability, and sometimes upon the cause of his mental retardation.

This discussion has been just a thumbnail sketch of the many factors parents must consider before making the decision of residential school versus living at home for their child. Every family situation is unique, each child has unique needs, so each set of parents must base their decision on their particular situation and their child's needs.

In making their decision, parents must place their child's needs and his happiness before their own wishes and sentiments.

The Search for the Right Residential School

If you decide that a residential school environment is best for your child, your next decision will be which one? Usually, this decision is preceded by, "How do I find out about schools of this type?"

The term "residential school" is used purposely throughout this discussion rather than "residential facility" or "home" or "institution," because school connotes teaching and training. This is the type of facility you will be looking for, not a place that offers only custodial care. Even the most severely mentally retarded child needs some teaching and therapy for stimulation and development so that he doesn't lose the ability he has or lose his interest in being a part of the world around him.

Most parents are only vaguely aware of the existence of such schools, until their search actually begins. The doctor or counselor who suggests placement should know of some schools and will usually make recommendations. Other parents who have children with similar handicaps are very good sources of information, especially those whose children are in schools. The local mental health service or the council for mentally retarded children will not only have a list of such schools, but is usually cognizant of the quality of and conditions in those that are nearby. The *Directory for Exceptional Children* (published by Porter Sargent, 11 Beacon Street, Boston, Massachusetts 02108) is a large book listing schools by state. Names of the directors and the mailing addresses as well as a brief description of each school is given, and although every school in each state is not included, the list is quite extensive. This book can be found in most libraries or can be ordered from the publisher for $14.00 (the 1971 price).

Another very valuable source of information is the *Directory of Residential Facilities for the Mentally Retarded*. This book is less expensive, costing only $2.50, and can be ordered from the American Association of Mental Deficiency, 5201 Connecticut Avenue N.W., Washington, D.C. 20001.

These directories and consultations with parents and people in the various agencies will provide you with names and locations and some idea of the services offered and the cost of the schools. But before making a definite choice, you should make every effort to visit the ones you are considering. Also (although some school administrators may not like this bit of advice, my concern is for you *parents*) , try to make at least one unannounced visit to the school you have selected before enrolling your child. This visit can and should be quite brief — you don't want to upset their routine, you only want to get some indication of the activities and conditions during an ordinary day. I feel that this is extremely important and completely justified on the parents' part, for this is your child you will be placing in the staff's care, and you have the right to know what to expect of his life there.

After you have inspected the school and observed the children (during a scheduled visit) , it is time then to talk about the details with the appropriate person, usually the director. You will want to know the cost — what is included in the basic tuition and what extra charges you will be expected to pay, such as medical expenses, laundry, and personal allowance. You will want to know about their testing program, what therapy and training your child will receive, and the qualifications and experience of the staff. Above all, you will want to know the purpose of the school as the administrators understand it, so you can determine whether this school offers what you want for your child. Is the main purpose directed toward development of each child's potential, their objective the health, care, and welfare of each child? Or is the school's purpose simply to provide an environment where those who cannot adjust to the normal society are protected — custodial care? Is too much concern centered on the children's progressive development at the expense of their social adjustment and happiness? And is the school well prepared for permanent residency should children need this? You will want to know, too, about the medical facilities and the staff doctors, especially if your child needs constant medical attention.

In many residential schools, particularly state supported schools, the fee or tuition is determined by the parents' ability to pay — sometimes based on taxable income, sometimes based on gross income. Make sure you know which is used before you fill out the forms, because the difference can be quite substantial.

You will probably be asked to sign a legal document whereby you consent to your child's being made a ward of the state (for state-supported schools), or the directors' of the school being made your child's legal guardian (usually in private schools). Don't be frightened by this — you will not be giving up your child, you will be protecting him by allowing the school officials the freedom to assume responsibility for his welfare and act in his behalf in the event of emergencies.

The only way that you will be "giving him up" or "putting him away" is through your own lack of attention to your child. Write to him even if he cannot read, for there will be someone to read your letters to him. Or, sometimes, you might send him a "picture letter," using pictures cut out of catalogues and magazines or drawings. By all means send snapshots of the family to him at frequent intervals. Letters and pictures will not make your child homesick, but will serve to reaffirm his sense of belonging to his family. Visits home are important, but usually it is not wise to make them too frequent or too long, for unless he is at the school for a limited period of time for training, the school is his home. Receiving presents is as necessary for a child living in a residential school as for any other children you may have at home, for to him gifts are visible proof of his family's love and thoughtfulness and assurance that they have not forgotten him.

If you decide to place your child in a residential school, at first the pain of having him away may be almost more than you can bear. You will worry about him — is he getting enough to eat? Is someone watching over him at night to cover him when he kicks his blankets off? Will someone care enough to comfort him when he cries? You will wonder, too, if he understands that you sent him to school because you love him so much and want the best for him, not because you love him less. However, time is a marvelous healer of pain, and when you visit him and see that he is happy there, you will know you made the right decision, that you have provided him with a life that is normal for him.

The Selection of the Right School

There are many criteria upon which you will judge the schools you are considering — physical appointments as to rooms and equipment, recreational facilities, ratio of staff to number of children enrolled, the kinds of therapies that are offered and the qualifications and experience of the staff, size of the school, distance from home, and cost, among others.

The most important criterion, however, and one which supersedes all others in importance is — the attitude of the staff members toward the children. Do the people who work with the children really like children? And this includes everyone from the cooks in the dining hall to the custodians and those who tend the lawns to the teachers and therapists and house mothers or dormitory fathers. Do they endeavor to provide a loving homelike atmosphere, where each resident is respected and accepted as the individual he or she is, with particular needs and abilities? Is the aim of the teaching and training to help each child develop his ability so that he can find dignity and purpose and achievement in his life? The general atmosphere of the school and the attitude of those who work with the children is far more important than the appearance of the building or the physical equipment, believe me.

Cost does not always determine quality. Do not believe that high costs of tuition is indicative of quality or assume that a private school is always better than a state-supported school.

I remember visiting one very expensive school during our search for the best school for our Kathy. Oh, it was beautiful in appearance — small dormitories surrounded by parklike grounds, extensive facilities for teaching and therapy; it seemed to be a dream situation at first glance. Then we saw the children. They were well dressed in sparkling clean uniforms, sitting quietly in chairs watching television in a large recreation room as they waited for the lunch bell to ring. At the ringing of the bell, those who could walk rose together and quietly filed out in neat lines, while stiffly starched, white-uniformed attendants efficiently helped those who needed assistance. All the time the children were eating, there was little talking and no laughing, and when the bell rang again announcing that lunchtime was over, they rose from the tables in unison, formed their lines again, and quietly marched back to their rooms for rest time. They were like little automatons, not children. Occasionally, we noticed a child shyly smiling, but no laughing did we hear during our entire three-hour visit, nor did we even once see a staff member put an arm around a child or show any sign of affection. The director, who was acting as our guide, explained, "Since we have children here with all degrees of retardation and many with physical handicaps, too, we find it best to keep them somewhat sedated. They learn better and are easier to handle." Oh, he could show us proof of remarkable progress some of the children had made, and the newest and most advanced teaching and therapy methods and equipment were used — but what about the children and their happiness?

The school we were finally fortunate in finding, where Kathy has been happy for eight years now, caught our approving attention from the moment we drove onto the campus. Again it was just before lunchtime. The campus resounded with an almost tangible aura of happiness as small groups of children of all ages played together, and the playground rang with many happy voices. The buildings were not fancy, but they were clean and the rooms were fairly attractively decorated. The classrooms were much more simply decorated and appointed than any public school classroom would be allowed to be; the physical therapy department was in the gymnasium, which also was used for all sorts of school functions such as dances, parties, and group sports. Grassy lawns were laced with well-worn paths; the trees shaded benches and swings, and flower beds were planted with the simple flowers children enjoy. There was a swimming pool — only waist deep — and a small chapel. The children were all happy and relaxed, open and free in their show of affection to each other and to the staff members, who never hesitated to return a greeting or a hug or attention in some manner. Lunchtime in the dining room was noisily chaotic, but every child who needed help eating was aided by a staff member or another child. The food was simple, but nutritionally well balanced. Unlike some of the other schools we visited, there was very little turnover in staff. Today, the school has grown in enrollment, and several endowments have provided for new dormitories, classrooms, and added staff. The atmosphere is still the same — that of a large, very happy family, all of whose members love and respect each other. Watching the development of our own daughter and several of her friends there over these past years, we have been amazed at the progress they have made in both physical and mental development. The school still lacks the therapy and teaching equipment we saw in other schools, but because the emphasis and interest is on each child's needs, equipment is not so important. (The tuition at this school is very reasonable, much less than at other schools, and only a little more than we would be charged at a state school.)

When you have decided that a residential school environment is best for your child, if he is capable of performing even simple tasks, another criterion you will want to consider in your choice of schools is the opportunity for him to earn a wage. Many schools have sheltered workshops for the residents; other types of work opportunity may also be offered, such as helping with the laundry or in the kitchen, assisting the teachers and housemothers, grounds-keeping and gardening, for which they may or may not be paid. If properly conducted with the interests, abilities, and the needs of the residents as the primary concern, such working programs can be of great benefit to those who participate. They have the satisfaction of being part of their particular society and being allowed to contribute to the needs of others. Being paid for a job they can perform gives them a sense of importance and purpose; being allowed to contribute their time and efforts gives them the security of feeling they belong and are part of this community in which they live.

The feeling of belonging is part of that homelike atmosphere upon which you will base your choice of schools for your child. He is very special to you, and knowing that he will be very special to those to whom you entrust him and that not only will his physical needs be well taken care of but that his need for love and understanding will not be ignored will ease the heartbreak of separation for you. You will then be assured that you are doing what is best for your child.

A Residential School Is Not Always the Best Decision

For many mentally retarded children, residential school is not the best environment. For many, it is best that they continue to live at home, or return home after a limited stay in a residential school for special training. Hundreds of thousands of parents are learning each day that they can give their mentally retarded children much happier and more meaningful lives at home. Many parents are learning, too, that their mentally retarded children can bring them great happiness and can enrich the family relationships.

There are many sources of help for parents whose mentally

retarded children are at home. Parents' groups can be of tremendous assistance to parents of children handicapped by any disability, and particularly so when a child is living within the family circle. Not only do parents find great solace in discussing their problems with other parents who have experienced similar problems, but also the exchange of such information often opens other avenues to sources of help. Also, through the combined efforts of these groups, effective action for improving existing facilities and services can be accomplished.

Caring for any child who is handicapped can be difficult, but parents whose children are mentally retarded usually find their responsibilities most burdensome. One of the new types of services is Respite Care for the Retarded. This program provides short-term care (frequently in public-supported facilities) for children and counseling for the parents. It is not yet available in all communities, and the kinds of services offered vary — but, at least, attention is now being paid to the needs of parents.

Services provided through this government-sponsored program include, under "Services Performed in the Home," housekeeping services — temporary, qualified help during family crises as well as baby sitters trained to work with physically handicapped and mentally retarded persons. "Services Performed Outside the Home" include: foster homes, temporary-care homes, family-group homes (usually four to six retarded children of similar age and level of development), group homes for older retarded individuals, halfway houses that serve as an interim, protected environment between residential school and return to the family or community, and state residential facilities for short-term stays for training or treatment or for trial separation for periods of family crisis or for family relief from the stress of caring for the child (in other words, for vacations when a handicapped child would be unable to go along with the rest of the family).

To learn more about this program, check with your local

health department or your state child welfare office. An excellent discussion and description of the program and a listing by states of facilities which offer these services can be found in the booklet, *Respite Care for the Retarded, An Interval of Relief for Families,* published in 1971 by the U.S. Department of Health, Education, and Welfare. To obtain this booklet, write to: Superintendent of Documents, U.S. Government Printing Office, Washington, D.C. 20402, and send 25¢ to cover cost.

There are several monthly magazines and newsletters put out by parents' groups which you might find very helpful. One of the best is published by the National Association for Retarded Citizens, an organization that has chapters in every state and serves as a clearing-house (or information center) and a referral agency to particular persons within specific agencies for help. The newspaper is *Mental Retardation News,* $3.50 per year for ten issues. The address is: National Association for Retarded Citizens, 2709 Avenue E, Arlington, Texas 76011. Other agencies and publications are listed in the Appendix under "Sources of Help."

Summary

Whatever your decision about your child's future may be — whether to keep him at home with the family or place him in a residential school — do not be afraid to trust your own judgment. So long as you can overlook your personal desires, your feelings of guilt, fear of criticism, and your fear that you will be denying your child your love, and think first of your child and his particular needs for happiness, you will make the right decision. Listen to your heart and be guided by your own ability to plan a life that is best for your child.

APPENDIX

Sources for Help

THERE ARE MANY sources of help available to parents whose children are handicapped. Among these sources are books written by parents about their experiences with their own handicapped children and others written by professional people explaining the causes and outlining treatments and therapy for the various handicapping disabilities. All these can help parents understand their children better and can also lead to a clearer understanding of their own feelings and adjustment problems.

Other sources offer information for the care and treatment of handicapped children, such as clinics, schools, and camps — often the most difficult information to gather. One of the frustrations most parents of handicapped children share is trying to find out where to go for help for their children — where are the clinics and schools and camps? Often, too, parents have a very real need for financial assistance for their child's care and do not know where to look for such information.

Information may be available through sources within the community — the doctors, counselors, teachers, and therapists who work with the child, or other parents who have children handicapped by similar disabilities. The local health office is another source of information, as is the office of the local medical society, nearby colleges and universities, public school counselors and/or principals, and the local Family Service office. Child welfare departments of the state governments are clearing-houses for information about services offered within the states.

These are all good and valuable sources, but sometimes parents wish to have information that is more specific to their particular needs, or they wish information of a broader scope or more expedient answers. Sometimes, too, parents prefer the anonymity of written correspondence rather than the personal involvement of telephone or face-to-face conversation. So, for these reasons, I have selected some of the agencies and sources of information I feel will be helpful. The list is not complete, but it is a place to start. Because the addresses are given for the various agencies and for the written information, help for you is really only a postage stamp away.

Some of the books suggested are regrettably out of print and are only readily available through libraries; others can be found in bookstores and public libraries. (If your library does not have a particular book, ask the librarian to locate it for you.) Our U.S. Government Printing Office is a very rich source of information and all too often disregarded — the pamphlets offered are very inexpensive, well written, and usually very comprehensive.

Books that May Help You Understand Your Emotions

Ayrault, Evelyn West. *You Can Raise Your Handicapped Child.* New York: G. P. Putnam's Sons, 1964. (Out of print, but still found on many library shelves. Very helpful and encouraging.)

Brutten, Milton; Richardson, Sylvia O.; Mangel, Charles. *A Parent's Book about Children with Learning Disabilities.* New York: Harcourt, Brace, Jovanovich, Inc., 1973.

Egg, Dr. Maria. *When a Child is Different: A Basic Guide for Parents and Friends of Mentally Retarded Children.* New York: The John Day Company, 1964.

French, Edward L., and Scott, J. Clifford. *Child in the Shadows: A Manual for Parents of Retarded Children.* New York: J. B. Lippincott Company, 1960. (Out of print, but very good — worth looking for.)

Hart, Jane, and Jones, Beverly. *Where's Hannah? A Handbook for Parents and Teachers of Children with Learning Disorders.* New York: Hart Publishing Company, 1968.

Hewett, Shiela. *Family and the Handicapped Child.* Chicago: Aldine-Atherton, Inc., 1970.

Katz, Alfred H. *Parents of the Handicapped.* Illinois: Charles C. Thomas, Publisher, 1961.

Koch, R., and Dobson, J. C. *The Mentally Retarded Child and His Family.* New York: Brunner/Mazel, 1971.

Love, Harold D. *Parental Attitudes toward Exceptional Children.* Illinois: Charles C. Thomas, Publisher, 1970. (Primarily concerns parents of mentally retarded children, but helpful to parents of any handicapped child.)

McDonald, Eugene T. *Understand Those Feelings.* Pittsburgh: Stanwix House, 1962.

Ross, Alan O. *The Exceptional Child in the Family.* New York: Grune and Stratton, 1964.

White, Robin. *Be Not Afraid: The Story of a Tragically Afflicted Child and His Stubbornly Courageous Family.* New York: The Dial Press, 1972.

Wing, Lorna. *Autistic Children: A Guide for Parents.* New York: Brunner/Mazel, 1971.

Books to Help You Understand and Help Your Child

Aryault, Evelyn West. *Helping the Handicapped Teenager Mature.* New York: Association Press, 1971.

Cruickshank, W. M. *Cerebral Palsy: Its Individual and Community Problems.* Illinois: Charles C. Thomas, Publisher, 1970.

Cruickshank, W. M. *Psychology of Exceptional Children.* New Jersey: Prentice-Hall, Inc., 1963.

Faber, Nancy W. *The Retarded Child.* New York: Crown Publishers, 1968.

Kirk, Samuel A. *Educating Exceptional Children.* Boston: Houghton Mifflin Company, 1962.

Lerner, Janet W. *Children with Learning Disabilities.* Boston: Houghton Mifflin Company, 1971.

Government Publications

This is a selected list of those I have found particularly informative. New information is being printed almost daily, so if you order any of these listed, you may want to ask for a recent listing of publications of the Children's Bureau of the U.S. Department of Health, Education, and Welfare.

Address your requests to:

SUPERINTENDENT OF DOCUMENTS

U.S. GOVERNMENT PRINTING OFFICE

WASHINGTON, D.C. 20402

Money orders and personal checks payable to "Superintendent of Public Documents" are accepted in payment. Time of delivery is from two to four weeks, usually, and a money order may speed delivery.

"Activity Centers for Retarded Adults," #4000–00284, 70¢.

"Childhood Leukemia: A Pamphlet for Parents," #1741–0041, 25¢.

"Facts about Autism," #1724–00259, 10¢.

"Learning Disabilities due to Minimal Brain Dysfunction: Hope through Research," Public Health Service Publication #16–46, 20¢.

"Maternal and Child Health Service Programs, Administering Agencies and Legislative Base," DHEW Publication #72–500, no charge. (Lists regional offices and state agencies responsible for administration of Maternal and Child Health and Crippled Children's services.)

"Mental Retardation Financial Assistance Programs of the Department of Health, Education, and Welfare," #1700–0084, 40¢.

"Mental Retardation, Its Biological Factors: Hope Through Research," DHEW Publication # (NIH) 72–155, 25¢.

"The Mentally Retarded Child at Home," Children's Bureau Publication #374, 35¢.

"Mental Retardation Activities of HEW," #1700–97, 20¢.

"Mongolism (Down's syndrome) : Hope through Research," PHS Publication #720, 10¢.

"Programs of the Maternal and Child Health Service," DHEW Publication # (HSM) 72–5005, 20¢.

"Publications of the Maternal and Child Health Service," DHEW Publication # (HSM) 71–5004, 20¢.

"Respite Care for the Retarded: An Interval of Relief for Families," (SRS-RSA) #174, 25¢.

"Services for Crippled Children," PHS Publication #2137, 20¢. (List of State and Federal agencies and addresses.)

Directories for Facilities and Services for Handicapped Children

Directory for Exceptional Children. Porter Sargent, 11 Beacon Street, Boston, Massachusetts 02108. (One of the Sargent Handbook Series that lists information concerning special education facilities and programs. Others in the series are: *The Underachiever* — guide to tutorial, remedial, diagnostic, and academic resources; *The Gifted: Educational Resources* — a survey of public and private facilities for education; and *Summer Camps and Summer Schools* — a reference source of summer programs, including those for exceptional children. Also, a bureau is maintained to provide parents with information concerning schools and camps. On request, a form will be sent to be completed with data that will be helpful in furnishing pertinent and helpful suggestions as to facilities. The 1971 cost of the *Directory* is $14.00; most public libaries have copies.)

Directory of Facilities for the Learning-Disabled and Handicapped, Careth Ellingson and James Cass, editors. Harper and Row Publishers, Inc., 10 East 53rd St., N.Y., N.Y. 10022. 1972, $15.00 hardbound; $6.95 paperback.

Directory of Residential Facilities for the Mentally Retarded. American Association of Mental Deficiency, 5201 Connecticut Avenue N.W., Washington, D.C. 20015. 1968, $2.50.

Help for the Handicapped Child, Florence Weiner. McGraw-Hill Book Company, 330 West 42nd Street, New York, New York 10036. 1973, $7.95. (Lists the general types of services available through state and national organizations.)

"A Selected Guide to Government Agencies Concerned with Exceptional Children," and, "A Selected Guide to Public Agencies Concerned with Exceptional Children," U.S. Government Printing Office, 65¢. Both may be ordered from: Special Education IMC RMC Network, 1411 South Jefferson Davis Highway, Suite 928, Arlington, Virginia 22202.

Social and Rehabilitation Services for the Blind, Richard E. Hardy and John G. Cull. Charles C. Thomas, Publisher, 301–327 East Lawrence Avenue, Springfield, Illinois. 1972, $15.75.

Some Agencies and Organizations that Offer Services to Handicapped Children and Their Parents

American Foundation for the Blind, 15 West 16th Street, New York, New York 10011. Serves as a clearing-house for information about blindness. Offers in-print publications; literature printed in large type, in braille, or recorded. Also offers field consultation, research, and personal referrals to other agencies.

Association for Children with Learning Disabilities, 220 Brownsville Road, Pittsburgh, Pennsylvania 15210. Concerns children and youths who have normal intelligence, but are hindered in learning because of perceptual, conceptual, or coordinative disabilities.

Closer Look, Box 1492, Washington, D.C. 20012. Special education information center, sponsored by the Bureau of Education for the Handicapped, U.S. Office of Education. Information supplied to parents and others about facilities serving handicapped children in their localities. (Also, information supplied for those interested in careers in special education.)

Council of Organizations Serving the Deaf, 4201 Connecticut Avenue, N.W., Suite 210, Washington, D.C. 20008. Among other services, a clearing-house and contact point for information and combined services of national organizations serving deaf persons.

Human Growth, Inc., 307 5th Avenue, New York, New York 10016. Begun by parents and friends of children with growth problems. Among other services, opportunities for contact with other families with children with growth problems and disabilities, financial aid for medical help.

Muscular Dystrophy Association of America, Inc., 1970 Broadway, New York, New York 10019. While its principle purpose is to foster scientific research into the cause and cure of muscular dystrophy and education among public and professionals, services are rendered to patients with the disease.

National Association of Hearing and Speech Agencies, 919 18th Street, N.W., Washington, D.C. 10006. Although the majority of the services are conducted through some two hundred local chapters, the national office does serve as an information center for the location of the local chapters.

National Association for Retarded Citizens, 2709 Avenue E East, Arlington, Texas 76011. Although each state has an organization to coordinate the activities of the chapters within that state, the national office serves as an information center and a referral agency — referral to local chapters and to particular persons within specific agencies in each state. Publishes a newspaper, *Mental Retardation News,* subscription rate $3.50 per year for ten issues.

The National Easter Seal Society for Crippled Children and Adults, 2023 West Ogden Avenue, Chicago, Illinois 60612. Offers a wide range of services, including: research into causes and cures of disabilities, education of the general public, direct services for crippled children and adults through hospitals and clinics. While members are the local chapters, information as to the locality of the chapters is given upon request.

National Multiple Sclerosis Society, 257 Park Avenue South, New York, New York 10010. Provides services to ms patients and their families, among many other services and functions. Information given upon request about local groups.

National Society for Autistic Children, 621 Central Avenue, Albany, New York 12206. Among other functions, serves as an information center for the exchange of news about behavior management techniques, research projects, schools, camps, and recreational services in the United States.

State Crippled Children's Services. Each state works in conjunction with the federal government to provide services, such as free diagnostic services available to all children brought to their clinics, help for parents with financial planning for treatment and care. May assume part or all of the cost, depending upon child's need, family resources, and availability of funds.

Services for children under twenty-one include orthopedic or plastic treatment (cleft palate, club feet, and chronic conditions affecting muscles, bones, and joints) based on parents' ability to pay, funds, et cetera.

Information about addresses and services offered in your state may be obtained from: Director, Maternal and Child Health Service, Health Services and Mental Health Administration, 5600 Fishers Lane, Rockville, Maryland 20852. (Also listed in the pamphlet, *Maternal and Child Health Service Programs*.)

United Cerebral Palsy Association, Inc., 66 East 34th Street, New York, New York 10016. Many functions and services. Local services are administered through local and state affiliated chapters and clinics. National office furnishes information upon request about the location of chapters and clinics and services offered.

There are many other very good organizations and agencies; these listed are either representative or ones with which I have had personal contact. Don't ever feel you are alone and have no one to whom you can turn for help and understanding. Whatever your child's handicap may be, there are other parents who have also experienced anxieties and confusion similar to yours. Wherever you may live, help for your child and for you is available.

INDEX

Index